WORDPLAY

Origins, Meanings, and Usage of the English Language

Robertson Cochrane

University of Toronto Press
Toronto Buffalo London

© University of Toronto Press Incorporated 1996
Toronto Buffalo London
Printed in Canada

ISBN 0-8020-7752-8

∞

Printed on acid-free paper

Canadian Cataloguing in Publication Data

Cochrane, Robertson, 1937–1995
   Wordplay : origins, meanings, and usage of the
   English language
   Based on two columns, "Word play" in The Globe and Mail
   and "Verbum sap" in Verbatim, the language quarterly.
   Includes bibliographical references and index.
   ISBN 0-8020-7752-8
   1. English language – Etymology – 2. English language –
   History. I. Title.
   PE1574.C63 1996   422   C96-930402-1

© *Verbatim: The Language Quarterly* for the following: 'Speaking of the ineffable,'
'My tainted ain't,' 'Niggles in a haystack,' 'The media is the message', and ''Ard
line.' Used by permission.

University of Toronto Press acknowledges the financial assistance to its
publishing program of the Canada Council and the Ontario Arts Council.

CONTENTS

FOREWORD

Sad to relate, most of those who take it upon themselves to write about language – linguists, in particular – are neither artists nor even artisans when it comes to style and imagination in their own inditements. It is therefore an unalloyed delight to see Robertson Cochrane's cogent commentaries captured in book form, a less transitory medium than the periodicals in which they originally appeared.

Cochrane's articles for the *Globe and Mail* were first brought to my attention by several perceptive readers in Canada; after reading a few, I wrote to ask if he would become a contributor to *Verbatim: The Language Quarterly*. He agreed and from then on we published an original piece by him in each issue.

Of course, writing well is only half the task; one must also have something to say. Owing to the vastness of the English language, it is impossible to believe that one would run out of things to say about its myriad aspects. Indeed, the scholarly journals have been overflowing with turgid prose for decades, and it is particularly refreshing to know that comment on virtually any aspect of language can still be offered in language that, glowing with respectability, cleaving to the well-turned phrase, punctuated by the provocative pun, can be so engagingly presented.

Whether Cochrane turns his attention to the punctuation of real estate advertising, to the zoomorphological reflexes of *crab-grass, dandelions*, or *foxglove*, to the jargon of the education(al)ists (as contrasted with educators), to anagrams, or to the meaninglessness of advertising copywriters' semantic distortions, his readers may be sure of an incisive, knowledgeable opinion –

which, I am sure, is shared by many of them – expressed in language that is a model of clarity and reflects at once sophistication and humour.

From the foregoing, any reader might correctly divine that I am an everlasting devotee of Robertson Cochrane's, whose writings deserve the widest readership among all those who love and cherish language.

Laurence Urdang, Editor
Verbatim: The Language Quarterly
Old Lyme, Connecticut,
and Aylesbury, Buckinghamshire

PREFACE

'Sir: I hesitate to trespass upon your space yet again,' wrote the great economist John Maynard Keynes in a letter to the editor of the London *Times* in 1925. 'This most fundamental problem of modern economic society requires a wider flight of thought and speech than I can expect you to accommodate. Confined within the birdcage of a column, one can but hop helplessly from one small perch to another.'

Professor Keynes, of course, was arguing a momentous issue of public economic policy, a field in which I would not dare to tread. I can sympathize, however, with the eminent Baron Keynes regarding the minor but frequent fits of claustrophobia with which one is seized as a newspaper columnist. The implacable word count is an infinitely archer enemy than the inexorable deadline; and if your effort is trimmed on the editor's desk, you can be sure that a helpful reader will straighten things out with her own letter to the editor, usually beginning something like, 'Mr Cochrane has overlooked ...' or 'I should have thought Mr Cochrane would mention the obvious point ...'

But since I can't expect to have the entire weekend edition of the *Globe and Mail* or any other newspaper to myself, and because I cannot command the rubber chicken circuit the way Lord Keynes undoubtedly could, I must be content with a small cage called 'Word Play,' small perches and all. Well not entirely content perhaps. There are ways in which a dedicated verbomaniac can reach a wider audience without the close tether of an arbitrary column space; one of those ways is to publish a book.

In my first book, *The Way We Word*, I did not take full advantage of this comparative freedom. It was nothing more, nothing less than a collection of

'Word Play' columns, and a handful of other short essays I had earlier published in the *Globe*. This book is different; it is certainly based on the 'Word Play' columns, but many of them contain additional material written specially for this book (and often to fill in the very gaps caused by that bogeyman, space shortage). It also contains samples from another column I write in *Verbatim: The Language Quarterly*. This column is called 'Verbum Sap,' which, I'm sure all readers will know, is an abbreviation of *verbum sapienti, sat est*, or 'a word to the wise is sufficient.'

All of this, naturally, assumes that there is someone – quite a few someones, in fact – who care even one one-hundredth as much about words and language as I do. I believe it is a fair assumption. A minor dispute over the meaning or history of a word is as apt as any other issue to attract letters to the editor's desk, or a heated exchange on a phone-in radio program. The liveliest debate at a cocktail party is as likely to be over a neologism as it is over Canada's constitution, abortion, or the fortunes of the local professional sport franchise.

Oliver Wendell Holmes once said that he would just as soon read his 'Dictionary' – he never referred to it without a capital initial – as any book of poetry. Personally, I think poetry needs a little more organization than the alphabetization afforded by a dictionary. But it is true that most words are art. That is to say, the vast majority of words in our vocabulary, those we know and use, and those awaiting discovery, began as pictures visible only to the mind's eye. It is truly astonishing, verging on the miraculous, that so many scenes of magic, whimsy, happiness, and despair can be conjured up by arranging only a few of twenty-six little symbols.

What is also a matter of some wonderment to me is the depth and breadth of debt I owe to so many people who helped me put this book together. Most of this assistance came from people who had no idea their support, their ideas, and their critiques would have some bearing on a book. Most of this moral and material support came from friends and colleagues and loved ones in the context of a single 'Word Play' column, or in the form of a question about the meaning of a word. Assistance of a somewhat more concrete nature was given unstintingly by Phil Jackman and Constance Schuller, my editors at the *Globe and Mail*, and by Laurence Urdang, editor of *Verbatim*.

R.C.

FABLES AND FOLKLORE

A search for the origins of popular expressions featuring proper names uncovers some interesting stuff – and a little bit of nonsense. It also leaves room for other opinions.

OF CHARLEY HORSES AND BETTY MARTIN

THE MAIL HAS AGAIN BEEN LADEN WITH WEIGHTY WORD questions. Some perplexed readers have been kind enough to let me share the burden of their puzzlement over certain proper names in popular expressions.

Among the latest bunch of bafflers was one from Reginald G. McAllan of Oakville, Ontario. He wondered about the origin of 'All my eye and Betty Martin,' a phrase still heard in Britain, but whose shorter, older versions, 'All my eye!' or just 'My eye!,' may be more familiar to North Americans. They all denote a sceptical 'humbug!' or an emphatic 'no way!' and they have stumped etymologists for well over two hundred years.

They stumped me too, but the search turned up some interesting stuff – and nonsense.

One story has it that a British sailor heard someone in an Italian church begin a prayer with *O, mihi, beate Martine*, which translates from Latin roughly as 'Oh, help me, blessed Martin.' According to this story, the sailor thought he heard 'All my eye and Betty Martin,' and then successfully spread it far and wide as a synonym for 'balderdash.' Incidentally, St Martin is the patron saint of drunkards – to be 'Martin-drunk' is to be particularly pie-eyed – so who knows what the supplicant may actually have been saying.

Only slightly less implausible is the tale recounted in 1914 by Dr L.A. Waddell in *The Phoenician Origin of Britons, Scots and Anglo-Saxons*. According to this story, the original prayer was *O mihi Brito Martis* – Britomartis being a Cretan goddess whose name meant 'sweet maid.' The theory here is that Britomartis's cult was associated with the sun-cults of the Phoenicians, who carried on early trade with Britons in Cornish tin.

Nigel Rees, in his *Dictionary of Word and Phrase Origins*, suggests there was a late-eighteenth-century actress named Betty Martin, whose favourite expression was said to be 'My eye.' So her name got added to the phrase for emphasis. Rees also speculates that Betty Martin may have been rhyming slang for 'fartin',' adding the element of empty wind to the exclamation.

Shirley Grant of Toronto was aching to know where *charley horse* was foaled, and this one turned out to be a bit of a nightmare too. The most popular theory is that it came from the name of a lame horse that pulled a grass-roller at Chicago's Comiskey Park baseball stadium in the 1890s. The trouble is, there are written examples of it dated 1888 and 1889, the context of which makes it clear that the expression was already familiar, thus much older.

There is another, iffier speculation. About two centuries before *peelers* and *bobbies* (British policemen named after Sir Robert Peel, around 1830), English constables became known as *Charleys* after King Charles I, who had responded to a crime wave by beefing up the night watch in London. This nickname supposedly hobbled across the Atlantic, and because leg cramps were an occupational hazard for watchmen, gimpy *Charleys* in the United States were said to be sore from 'riding Charley's horse.' From there, the expression spread to other occupations, and took firm root in baseball and other sports.

You can take your pick of the two explanations, make up one of your own, or just suffer plain old cramps, sprains, and bruises.

Richard Peart of Red Deer, Alberta, said a column about middens, shambles, and other messes (see page 16) reminded him of an expression his mother used to describe untidy quarters. 'When she passed my room,' Mr Peart wrote, 'she would say it looked like "who shot Aggie."' She also used this epithet when referring to the rat-nest or bedhead appearance of my sisters' hair in the morning.'

Catch-phrases are replete with Toms, Jacks, and Dicks, and even Berthas and Bettys, but Aggies are decidedly unubiquitous in this field. The only one I could find was a nineteenth-century schoolboy phrase, 'going to see Aggie,' one of approximately umpteen thousand genteelisms for going to the euphemism. But this doesn't explain the 'shot' part, and there is no obvious connection with the agate playing marble or an agricultural college student, both called 'aggies.'

Could it be that the *Aggie* here is not a proper name and the object of the verb, but rather an adverb – say, a corruption of *agee* meaning 'off-kilter,' or *agley*, a Scottish word for 'awry'? This would fit the messy context, and the sense then could be 'who fired a cannon off-target and hit your room by mistake?'

That's just a wild guess, and both Richard Peart and I would be grateful to hear from any smart-Aleck reader who can ease our Aggie-nizing.

———————————   •   •   •   ———————————

Weddings used to be called 'bride-ales' because much beer was consumed. Here we also discover how a month of sweet drinking gave us 'honeymoon' and how an overdose ended Attila's career.

A CASE OF ALTARED STATES? AISLE SAY!

DURING HER PROGRESSIVE CONSERVATIVE LEADERSHIP CAMPAIGN, contender Kim Campbell said her honeymoon was over before the marriage vows were muttered. 'I always said I expected to be left at the altar by the media,' the jilted Ms Campbell said in reference to the somewhat less than ardent news coverage she was getting. 'And here I am, wilted flowers in hand.'

The non-blushing non-bride may have mistaken a knee-jerk reaction for a bended-knee proposal, but in her choice of metaphor she displays an almost poetic sense of timing. This is June, after all, named for Juno, the Roman goddess of marriage, and the month in which weddings, according to old Roman superstition, are 'good to the man and happy to the maid.'

Almost as common as June weddings are nuptial how-to books, providing more or less useful tips on virtually everything to do with marriages, including how to make them happy and/or long ones. One little-addressed area, in spite of loud and incessant demand, is the terminology of matters matrimonial. This is a modest and necessarily incomplete attempt to redress this lamentable lacuna.

Since the whole shebang goes under the heading of *matrimony*, or 'mother-ment,' it's no surprise that the star of the show has always been the bride. In Old English she was a *bryd*, which was related to a Gothic German word meaning 'daughter-in-law.' This may have been rooted in the Indo-European *bhreu*, 'to brew or cook,' which menial task was usually carried out in primitive times by the daughter-in-law. That old *bhreu* is thought also to have bred *breed*, *brood*, *breathe*, *bread*, *broth*, *burn*, *brand*, and *brimstone*.

The word *bridal* is no simple adjectival extension like *adjectival*. Long before champagne toasts, the newly knotted couple sealed their vows with honest ale, and the guests followed suit with Gusto, an early best-selling brand of suds. Besides being a drink, the Old English *ealu*, later *ale*, was also the word for a drinkfest, and a *bride-ale* or *bridal* was the marriage celebration itself. It wasn't until about 1600 that it joined the ranks of other Latin-based modifiers ending in *-al*, such as *natal* and *mortal*.

Today's *bridegroom* is the product of that quaint process of word formation called folk etymology. He was originally a *brydguma*, the second element being an Old English word for 'man.' It evolved into *gome*, but became obsolete in Middle English, when it was replaced by the similar, and more familiar, *grome*. This word, whose main sense at the time was 'servant' or 'stable boy,' but which was also used commonly to mean 'lad,' became our *groom*.

If marriage these days seems statistically a bit of a gamble, there is some historical reason. The Old English noun *wed*, now obsolete, was a security deposit or gage. It was influenced by a raft of Germanic words meaning 'pledge' or 'wager.' The modern German word for 'bet' is *wette*.

Until the 1600s it was not uncommon to put something *in wed*, which meant to pawn or mortgage it. But to *lay wed* was to put down a stake in a game or wager, and *wed* as a verb for 'wager' or 'stake' persisted in English until the seventeenth century. A northern and Scottish version, *wad*, is still used for 'bet.'

Something often pledged, promised, or *wedded* was one's hand in marriage, and the sense gradually narrowed to include only matrimonial things. There are today such things as marriage-brokers, but at one time a *wedbreaker* was an adulterer. And the conjugal couch was once known as the *wed-bed*.

The gerund *wedding* is a strong modern survivor, but other forms of the verb are rarely heard outside the marriage rites and in the figurative sense of being 'wedded' to an idea or cause.

The lock in *wedlock* has nothing to do with fasteners or hanks of hair and, contrary to popular belief, does not denote a permanence or fastness. It is the only modern survivor of an Old English suffix, *-lac*, which represented merely a condition, practice, or action.

There are some etymological chicaneries in our marriage customs, too.

Some language fogeys still make pedantic protestation against the expression 'walking down the aisle,' arguing that an aisle, from the French *aile*, or 'wing,' is properly one of two passages on either side, or wing, of a church. Brides and grooms traditionally traipse down the *nave*, or central walkway, according to this reactionary credo – whose only flaw is that it's obsolete by about two and a half centuries.

Since about 1750, *aisle* has commonly applied to any walking space separating seating areas in a church, theatre, concert hall, meeting room, and, later still, movie house, train, plane, or bus. If puffed-up purists want to insist on outdated sense restrictions, they should in consistency also hold out for Samuel Johnson's recommended spelling, *aile*, or the more common spelling during his day, *isle*.

Aisle has always been a knotty word, hardly auspicious for the path that bears the first few steps in the great journey of matrimony.

In Middle English it was *ele* or *hele*, a straightforward borrowing from the Old French *ele*, which came from the Latin *ala*, 'wing.' This was etymologically in tune with the sense of a passage running along the side or wing of a building.

The English spelling tumbled through *ille*, *eill*, and *eyle*, so similar to the contemporary word for 'island' that it became one and the same: *ile* or *yle*, and later *isle*. The modern spelling is an amalgam of the French *aile* and the English *isle*. The modern sense, however, contains yet another confusion – with the French *allée*.

Guests are plopped into their pews on either side of this island, alley, or wing by an *usher*, a much-mangled medieval word traced to the Latin *ostium*, 'door.' Among its many spelling variants was *husher*, neatly describing the role of some ushers.

When woman and man *plight their troth* (pledge their truth), they may avoid the aisle business altogether by *eloping* (probably not from the Dutch *lopen*, 'to run,' as is commonly supposed, but from an Anglo-French form of 'leap'). If they choose to get churched, they may also opt for the old custom of having the *banns* read. *Bann*, used only in the plural now, is the same word as *ban*, another French loan-word that originally meant not only a proscription but also a public proclamation, such as a call to arms by a feudal lord.

A ban could be a curse or, worse, excommunication enunciated by an authorized cleric. But as early as the twelfth century it also described an announcement of an intended marriage, with the proviso that the union could be stopped by anyone with a legitimate objection. The traditional reading of the banns for three successive Sundays is now customarily truncated to one terse but tension-producing line in the marriage rite, after which everyone is told to button his or her lip, or 'hold your peace.'

From one of the early feudal senses, *ban* developed an adjectival meaning, 'of or belonging to a compulsory feudal service.' It acquired the further sense of 'available for community use' – such as a common grist mill, or the village pump. From there the adjective – *banal* – degraded to 'commonplace, trite, or trivial.'

The knot duly tied, the bridal pair used to be pelted with raw rice, a custom that pleased pigeons but peeved sextons, who had to clean up the nuptial debris. The birds were probably disappointed and the janitors unappeased when the cereal flak was replaced by tiny pieces of paper called *confetti*. In its native Italian, *confetti* meant 'bon-bons' or 'candy,' paper imitations of which were thrown during carnivals. Our words *confection* and *comfit* are related.

That sweet note brings us to *honeymoon*. Thomas Blount's 1656 *Glossographia* spelled it *hony-moon*, and said it 'applyed to those marryed persons that love well at first, and decline in affection afterwards; it is hony now, but it will change as the Moon.' The best guess is that this stems from an ancient German ritual requiring the new couple to imbibe a potent honey-based mead every day for the first month – or moon – of their married life, so as to ensure a long and happy one. Attila the Hun, or perhaps the Hungover, is said to have observed this custom so assiduously that he drank himself to death on the first night.

That was one wedding that didn't come off without a hitch. After the official one, that is.

• • •

Reduplication is a linguistic phenomenon rife with rhyme but often bereft of reason. It's probably rooted in the 'mamas' and 'dadas' of baby talk, but it was no infant who invented 'fender-bender.'

OKEY-DOKEY, HERE'S A REAL HODGE-PODGE

PERHAPS BECAUSE THE PICNIC DIN-DIN FEATURED A POTPOURRI OF yum-yum things for the tum-tum – won-ton, cous-cous, Pizza Pizza, mai-tais, and some super-duper bon-bons – my companion idly wondered why language has so many rhyming, alliterative expressions such as the ones with which this higgledy-piggledy paragraph is chock-a-block.

My friend conjectured that a high proportion of these linguistic gew-gaws start with the eighth letter of the alphabet – helter-skelter, hoity-toity, hurdy-gurdy, hurly-burly, holus-bolus – a hunch later borne out, but unexplained, by a hasty electronic hippety-hop through the pages of the *Oxford English Dictionary*. Deeper delving failed to solve the hugger-mugger of the *h*-words, but it did unearth a whole hodge-podge of other fascinating *hitheracs and skitheracs* (a Yorkshire dialect doublet meaning 'odds and ends').

The phenomenon, known as reduplication, is a field rife with rhyme but often bereft of reason. In part it may be a tenuous tendril to our Anglo-Saxon poetic past, where alliteration, not rhyme, was employed to add vim and vigour to verse. There may be something more primal in all this. Among our first utterances is the reduplicated 'mama,' just as it was for infants of the Indo-European tribes thousands of years ago. A baby's instinctive articulation of its longing for the nourishing breast gave us *mammal* and *mammalia*.

Linguists point out that reduplication occurs frequently in so-called primitive languages. You can see it in the Samoan skirt, *lava lava*, and the Hawaiian dish *laulau*, which is the word for leaf reduplicated. It's common in place-names such as Bora Bora and Pago Pago.

After we master 'mama' and 'dada' or 'papa,' our intellectual horizons expand rapidly to include such curiosities as 'bow-wows' and 'gee-gees.' Our early exposure to literature introduces characters like Henny-Penny and Turkey-Lurky, and when we can string our own sentences together we are pleased as punch to recite poems about Humpty-Dumpty and Jack Sprat, or to rattle off the riddle of Peter Piper and his pickled peppers.

We never really outgrow our penchant for these pairs. It was not likely children who wrought *riff-raff* in the Middle Ages or *zig-zag* in the 1700s. Adults probably fashioned *fuddy-duddy* at the turn of the century and later coined *killer-diller, boogie-woogie, fender-bender,* and anything *a-go-go.*

The obsession is not solely English. We adapted the French *pique-nique* for noshing in nature, and when we are head-over-heels with infatuation we borrow the Gallic *gaga,* or 'dotingly senile,' to describe our gape-mouthed giddiness. Closer to home, an Algonquian word for a tobacco mixture is the palindromic *kinnikinnik,* and an Eastern Canadian First Nations group goes by the name of 'allies,' or Micmac.*

Some ancient doublings lie hidden in everyday words. An Indo-European root *smer-,* 'to remember,' became *mer* in Latin. By a process of reduplication, this evolved into *memor,* 'mindful,' which gave English its *memory.* The echoic Sanskrit *maramara,* 'rustling sound,' was a precursor of the euphonious English word *murmur.*

Other common compounds mask fascinating origins. *Criss-cross* was at first 'Christ's cross,' a representation of which was printed at the front of medieval alphabet books. The alphabet was then commonly called the 'Christ-cross-row.'

Another term with a religious overtone is *hocus-pocus.* It probably came from a seventeenth-century English magician called Ochus Bochus, who used sham Latin to impress his audiences. But in 1694, John Tillotson, archbishop of Canterbury, alleged that *hocus-pocus* was an anti-Papist parody on the words *hoc est corpus* (this is [Christ's] body) of the Roman Catholic Eucharist.

The reduplication process is particularly prolific in dialect. In Scotland, there is the delightfully descriptive *glunch and gloom,* 'to sulk, whinge, or

---

* I was informed later that this Indian nation had changed its name to Mi'kmaq to more accurately reflect the aboriginal word.

grumble.' A little south, in Yorkshire, to *glop and gauve* means 'to stare stupidly or go gaga.' To be *mipsy-pimsey* in Devonshire is to be affectedly fastidious, and if you can't make up your mind in East Anglia, you may be called *quavery-mavery*.

A West Country word for unsteady or ill-balanced (or even cross-eyed) is *wee-wow*. In Shropshire, *kim-kam* means the same thing. For something that's totally awry, my all-time, no-nonsense, tried-and-true favourite is the Lincolnshire term *squetched and skywannocked*. And if that doesn't tickle you, that's okey-dokey and hunky-dory with me.

———————————   • • •   ———————————

The traditional work of the weaver has provided a rich tapestry of meanings in modern English, from subtle texts to tissues of lies to all things technical. Just make sure you don't lose the thread.

LIVING IN THE MATERIAL WORLD

OUR TEXT TODAY IS FROM A JOURNAL CALLED *HANDWOVEN*, A weavers' magazine published in Loveland, Colorado, sent in by 'Word Play' reader and webster Claire Coates, of Woodbridge, Ontario.

In it, columnist-publisher Linda Ligon unravels the knotted history of the word *loom*, tracing it back to the Old English word *geloma*, which denoted a tool or weapon, or any article used frequently. 'So you had Anglo-Saxon serfs going out and raking their fields with their looms,' Ms Ligon writes. In the fifteenth and sixteenth centuries, *lome* was a vulgar metaphor for 'penis,' as 'tool' still is; then it became an insulting epithet, also as 'tool' is still used today.

At various times, a *loom* was also a pail or a tub, a boat, and the shaft of an oar. Ms Ligon says the word also signified a breeze, a mist, a water bird, or one of those optical illusions that make things look bigger as they loom on the horizon, but these looms are not from the same etymological skein as the utensil-loom. Ditto for the verb *loom*, which is from a Germanic word meaning to 'move slowly.'

The first written record of the word as a weaver's apparatus was a reference to a 'lynyn lome' in the *Records of the Borough of Nottingham* of August 27, 1404. This is virtually the only surviving sense of the noun, and the word's history illustrates one of the main processes of semantic change, known as specialization, or narrowing of meaning. The opposite process is called extension or widening.

The word *text*, which we opened with, is a classic example of extension. *Text* has been traced back to an Indo-European root, *teks*, 'to weave or fabricate.' In Latin this became *texere*, also meaning 'to weave.' Then the extension process set in. The Latin word *textus* meant literally 'that which is woven' or a web, but broadened to include the style or 'tissue' of a literary work. In Old Northern French *tixte* meant the Scripture, but when *text* entered English in the fourteenth century it denoted anything written or printed.

From *textere* was also woven the Old French *tissu*, which we imported and gave approximately umpteen different spellings before settling on the modern *tissue*. At the outset, however, it had nothing to do with delicate paper products or biological substances. It was a rich cloth, interwoven with gold or silver. The figurative 'tissue of lies' was not flimsy or transparent, but rather an intricately 'woven' deceit.

Texture in English originally meant 'the process or art of weaving.' By the seventeenth century, its terms of reference broadened to include the character of a *textile* (i.e., 'woven') fabric. Before long, it extended to 'the constitution, structure, or substance of anything' – from soil and stucco, to temperament, music, and the *context* of literature – that is, the 'weaving' together of words and sentences.

Pretext has a complex and compelling warp and weft. The Latin verb *praetextere* meant literally 'to weave before' or 'to border,' then widened to 'to cloak, disguise, or pretend.' A *toga praetexta* was a Sunday-best suit with a woven border of showy purple. When the noun *pretext* gained currency in English in the sixteenth century, it stood for something intended to cover the true purpose, an excuse, pretence, or specious plea.

That Indo-European *teks* also spawned the Latin *tela*, signifying the web, net, or warp of a fabric. *Sub-tela* referred to the thread passing under the lengthwise 'warp,' or the finest thread. The adjective for this was *subtilis*, from which we derived *subtle*, although we experimented with many different spellings before settling on the present one. Chaucer's *Knight's Tale* speaks of 'The sharpe swerd ouer his heed / Hangynge by a *soutil* twynes threed.' Shakespeare's first folio had *subtil* and *subtle* evenly distributed; Milton used *suttle* in all of his poems except *Paradise Regained*, in which the modern spelling appears.

The ancient root *teks* also branched, via Greek, into *architect*, *technology*, *technique*, *tectonic*, and all things *technical*, perhaps in living *Technicolor*.

Weave and *web* are from the Indo-European *webh*, which meant 'to weave' and also 'to move quickly,' perhaps like the weaver's fingers. The first sense produced *woof* and *weft*, derivatives of the Old English *wefan*, 'weave.' It also developed into the Middle Low German *wafel*, 'honeycomb,' which in turn became our *wafer* and *waffle*. The back-and-forth movement of the weaver's hands was denoted by Old English *wafian*, which became *wave*; in Low German, the activity was denoted by the verb *wabbeln*, from which we derived *wobble*. The other ancient sense, that of quick movement, is reflected in the modern word *weevil*, from Old English *wifel*, a beetle whose chief trait was 'to move briskly.'

And I think that pretty well ties up most of the loose ends of this tangled tapestry.

———————————   •   •   •   ———————————

For some reason, many English words for rubbish come from the land of the Vikings. For a start, there's 'muck' and 'midden.' And in case you wondered, we're also talking 'trash.'

A LOAD OF SCANDINAVIAN GARBAGE

IT WASN'T SO MUCH THE ALLURING ALLITERATION THAT DREW ME to the headline 'Merits and Demerits of Metro's Middens.' It was the peculiar use of that evocative word *midden*.

The story was about the controversy over potential dump sites for Metropolitan Toronto's dregs and dross. *Midden* is a fine old Middle English word for a dunghill or a pile of kitchen waste. The closest things to it today are compost heaps, which are coming back into good odour, so to speak. But to picture a 'Metro midden' is to envisage a truly prodigious pile of coffee grounds and potato peels.

It is not a common word, *midden*. An informal survey revealed that familiarity with it is in direct proportion to the degree of Scottishness in the respondent. This explains why it was 'evocative' for me. My mother often used *midden* as a figurative descriptor of my admittedly less than immaculate room, and sometimes of me.

For some unapparent reason, many of our garbage words come to us from Scandinavian. *Midden* was dumped on English by the Danes, whose word for it was *mögdynge* (*mög*, 'muck,' and *dynge*, 'heap'; the latter is also cognate with *dung*). In fourteenth-century England this was rendered *medynge*, and it decomposed through *myding* and *myddin* before settling on its present spelling in the 1800s. Such a word was bound to be wielded allusively, and a classic was historian Charles Kingsley's 1859 reference to 'that everlasting midden which men call the world.'

We have already seen that the pungently expressive *muck* was a gift from the Scandinavians. They derived it from an Old Germanic word, *meuk*, or 'soft,' which has also been relayed to us as *meek*. Over the centuries we've used *muck* in reference to dung, dirt, clay, peat, filth, manure, medicine, unappetizing food, miscellaneous merchandise (*muck and truck*), excrement, hostile anti-aircraft fire, bad weather, and mud.

The hard-edged epithet *muckraker* was first used figuratively by John Bunyan in *Pilgrim's Progress* (1684) to describe someone preoccupied in the pursuit of worldly gain. It has come to mean any excessive interest in scandalous or immoral behaviour, and US president Teddy Roosevelt was the first to apply it to hyper-investigative journalists.

Trash is another old throwaway from the land of the trolls. Swedish *trasa* and Norwegian *trase* mean 'rags or tatters,' and a Norwegian dialect word *trask* stands for 'trash or baggage.' Icelanders have *tros*, which means 'fallen leaves and twigs.' In sixteenth-century English it covered twigs, splinters, hedge cuttings, straw, rags, and refuse in general.

Trash is the all-purpose word for household waste in most of the United States, and from that country also came the specialized term *white trash* for poor white Southerners. As a synonym for anything of little worth, *trash* gained fame when Shakespeare put into Iago's mouth the line: 'Who steals my purse steals trash.'

Garbage may have come from Old French *garbe*, 'sheaf,' because one of the early English meanings was the leaves and stems of grain chopped up for horse food. But that doesn't answer for an even earlier English use of the word for animal offal, and occasionally human entrails. *Garbage* seems to be the waste-word of choice for 'sanitary fill' in Canada, but it, like all of its cousins, has come to mean any worthless thing, material or immaterial.

When my mother wasn't condemning my room as a midden, my father was likening it to a *shambles*. This ancient and multifaceted word comes from the same root as the Modern German *schemel*, or 'stool.' The Anglo-Saxon *scamol* was a footstool or a counter for displaying goods or counting money. Later it narrowed to mean a table for showing meat for sale, and in its plural *shamells*, *shammoulles*, *chambulles*, and finally *shambles* broadened to mean a meat market, then a slaughter-house, then any scene of carnage and wholesale killing, such as a battlefield. The deterioration of meaning slowed and became less sanguinary in this century, and *shambles* has come to mean merely a condition of considerable disarray or just a plain mess. Or a midden.

——————————————— •   •   • ———————————————

Many numerical metaphors come with a variety of theories about their beginnings. But the experts are at sixes and sevens over the origin of the expression 'dressed to the nines.'

AT ODDS WITH A NUMBER OF NUMBERS

I
T'S OFTEN SAID THAT BASEBALL IS A NUMBERS GAME – NOT PITCHER versus batter, but an infinite series of showdowns between one set of statistical averages and another. Ordinal numbers play a big part too, as this item from the *Globe and Mail* sports page reveals: 'Darnell Coles ... hit his *first* career Fenway homer in the *second* [inning] on the *first* pitch with one out. It was the *second* of his career against Clemens. Joe Carter, who entered the game hitting .160 since May 26, hit his *second* in two days (No. 22) with one on in the *third*. It was his *17th* career Fenway homer and the *first* time he homered on successive days since June 26 and 27 at Milwaukee ...'

No wonder Abbot and Costello had trouble figuring out 'who's on first?'

English has umpteen numerical metaphors, many of which come with a suitcase full of folkloric theories about their origin. *Dressed to the nines* is one of them. A popular and superficially attractive explanation is that this was originally *to then eyen*, Middle English for 'to the eyes.' If you were dressed to the eyes, you were indeed fully garbed, maybe even overdressed. Eventually, say the folklorists, the *n* in the early definite article strayed over to the noun, a not uncommon phenomenon in word development. Some credence is lent to this by the fact that the earliest known mention of the numerical version had it as 'to the nine,' which is more in aural harmony with *eyen* than the modern plural is.

But there are problems with this. First, although it seems such a natural metaphor, there is no record of any Middle English predecessor of today's *to the nines*, or even of today's (*up*) *to the eyes*, meaning deeply involved or in debt. The earliest citation for the latter in the *Oxford English Dictionary* is

1778, and for the former 1787. If either expression had arisen in the medieval period, there would almost certainly be a recorded use before the late eighteenth century.

Second, when a word or expression mutates through folk-etymology, it usually changes from something archaic or obscure to something more familiar, but still contextually logical. A switch from *eyen* (eyes) to *nine(s)* makes no semantic sense.

Cobham Brewer may have come closer. His *Dictionary of Phrase and Fable* (1870) noted that nine was a mystical number. Among other things, it was the Trinity times three, often representing the 'nth' degree, or perfection. By this analogy, today's *dressed to the nines*, or elaborately togged out, adds up.

Mysteriously, the most recent edition of Brewer's popular reference work cites the *eyen* hypothesis and ignores the mystic-nine connection. It offers no explanation for the change.

Oxford doesn't even guess at the origin, content to give a definition – 'to perfection, to the highest degree or point,' which seems consonant with the early Brewer theory – plus ten citations. One of them is a quotation from the *Story of the Wiltshire Regiment* (1963), which offers this improbable stab: 'The 99th's sartorial perfection at this time [c. 1850] is said to have given rise to the expression "dressed up to the nines" as other regiments in Aldershot were constantly trying to achieve the same standard.'

So we're left at sixes and sevens.

Similarly perplexing is the expression *do a number on*, 'to do a disservice to,' or 'to hoodwink.' It is likely from show business, and may even be Canadian in origin. The earliest use I could find is from *Maclean's* of November 1974. From an article by Myrna Kostash, it's quoted in the *Third Barnhart Dictionary of New English*: 'In the bad, bleak old days, when I felt I was on my own among male relatives, male bosses, male lovers who were all, at one time or another, doing numbers on me, my only out – I thought – was celibacy.'

Reader Brian Fenoulhet of Etobicoke suggested that *do a number on* derives from the numerical nursery code expressions *number one* and *number two*. 'Reading the [Kostash] quotation, I was instantly reminded of the 1930s phrases for describing the micturation and defecation functions as Number One and Number Two,' Mr Fenoulhet wrote. Certainly, *do a number on* is similar, if not equivalent, to *dump on*, an expression that even more closely reflects the possible scatological beginnings. Note also the slang noun forms – *doggie do(o)*, and baby-talk *do-do*. Mr Fenoulhet's suggested derivation sounds highly plausible to me, although I have yet to find it in any reference work.

Ed Trump of Etobicoke came up with an odd request. He wanted me to do a number on four English phrases with a numerical affinity, and by an odd coincidence, they involved four consecutive odd numbers.

The first was *third world*. Oddly enough, defying the conventions of chronology, the third world was named first. At a conference in 1955, a Monsieur A. Sauvy coined the French term *tiers monde* for countries not politically aligned with either the capitalist or communist bloc, and the phrase quickly caught on in English as *third world*. Technically, this would have included such developed countries as Sweden and Switzerland, but it was clear from the start that the epithet referred to the poorer countries of Asia, Africa, and Latin America.

Worlds number one and two have been less unanimously defined, probably because both the capitalist and communist worlds insisted they were first. In 1974, Acting Premier Deng Xiaoping of China maintained that the first world consisted of the two superpowers, the United States and USSR, the second world was made up of other industrialized countries of any political persuasion, and the third world covered the developing nations.

This didn't sit well with such important countries as Britain, France, and Japan. The result was that hardly anyone ever spoke of the first and second worlds, but *third world* survived. Because it is sometimes used pejoratively, attempts have been made to make the distinction between 'haves' and 'have-nots' more neutral. The current favourite is 'north-south,' whose only flaws are imprecision, inaccuracy, and Euro-American hubris.

How about the *fifth estate*? In the beginning, there were three Estates of the Realm in Britain – the Lords Spiritual (bishops and such), Lords Temporal (barons, knights, etc.), and the Commons. The earliest reference to a 'fourth estate' is in Henry Fielding's *Covent Garden Journal* (1752), which mentions 'that very large and powerful body which form the fourth estate ... The Mob.'

In 1821, William Hazlitt called the notorious journalist-agitator William Cobbett a one-man fourth estate. Twenty years later, Thomas Carlyle quoted orator Edmund Burke as saying that in addition to the three traditional estates of parliament, the chaps in the press gallery formed a 'fourth estate more important far than they all.' The flattered press seized on this accolade, and the phrase has endured as a label for journalism.

In 1932, the *Times* of London noted that the exciting new electronic medium, radio, was being called 'the fifth estate.' The term has never had much currency, except in Canada, where the CBC television current affairs program, 'Fifth Estate,' has been running for more than twenty years.

The lucky digit seven figures in many metaphors, but in none of them so blissfully as *seventh heaven*. Since ancient times, heaven has denoted both the physical sky or firmament, and the spiritual abode of god(s) and decent but deceased mortals. In 1500 BC or so, Babylonian astronomers decided that each of the seven known planets (besides earth, but including the moon and sun) was surrounded by a spherical shell, or a 'heaven' of its own.

Successive discoveries raised the number to eleven, but the original notion of seven heavens embedded itself in Jewish theology, and later in Islam. The *seventh heaven* was reserved for God and the most exalted angels.

Most of us have to settle for an occasional sojourn on *cloud nine*. William and Mary Morris's *Dictionary of Word and Phrase Origins* says this metaphor for euphoria is based on the US Weather Bureau's classification of cloud types – the ninth or highest being the towering cumulonimbus. The difficulty with this theory is that it presupposes a widespread familiarity with weatherman jargon. In addition, cumulonimbus piles usually herald summer thunder and lightning, and often hailstorms – conditions not usually associated with elation.

Besides, the earliest quotations in the *Oxford English Dictionary*, from the 1950s, refer to 'cloud seven.' This may mean that *cloud nine* is the same as *seventh heaven*, which, based on current knowledge of the universe, really should be *eleventh heaven*. Odd, isn't it?

•   •   •

We often use two words that mean the same thing when one – or even none – would do. For instance, there's that phrase asking that the bearer be allowed to pass 'without let or hindrance.'

FINE AND DANDY PASS-PORT TO REDUNDANCY

H OW MANY PEOPLE ACTUALLY READ FINE PRINT? A FRIEND OF mine – a wise, witty, and altogether wonderful fellow who also happened to be the estimable editor of the *Globe and Mail* 'Word Play' column – is a sedulous scanner of the inconsequential. When he acquired a new passport, he noticed on the inside front cover a flowery-scripted message from the Secretary of State for External Affairs of Canada, in the name of Her Majesty.

The message is directed not at the passport holder but, presumably, to grim-faced immigration satraps from Blaine, Washington, to Ulan Bator, Mongolia. It politely and officiously implores them to allow the bearer to pass 'freely without let or hindrance.' Something about that phrase struck my perspicacious pal as redundant. And it is – prodigiously so.

The meaning would not be altered in any way, shape, or form – not one iota, jot, tittle, or smidgen – if it were over and done with at 'freely.' But, in the way of all pieces of paper ennobled by the term *document*, it goes over and above and beyond, adding words that are not only stilted, but also superfluous, excessive, gratuitous, dispensable, uncalled for, and – first and foremost – pure and simple drivel.

Let is one of those Janus words, or contronyms, which have two virtually opposite meanings. Its common modern sense is 'to allow or permit.' The other, synonymous with *hindrance*, comes from Old English *lettan*, 'to delay, impede, or laten.' An early health-food freak, Thomas Cogan, used it this way when he wrote in 1584: 'Much meat eaten at night, grieveth the stomack, and letteth naturall rest.' The noun form survives in racquet games, when something interferes with play, and in the rococo rhetoric of Canadian passports and other documentese.

There are no hard and fast rules and regulations, but redundant couplets – also called pleonasms, tautologies, and nonsense – seem to all intents and purposes to be part and parcel of the bag and baggage of the language of law. Under the terms and conditions of most leases, you are entitled to both peace and quiet, which is only right and proper, or meet and fit. Save and except you pay your rent when it's due and payable, you could render the contract null and void, soon after which you could find yourself not only out of house and home, but also out on the sidewalk with your goods and chattels (the latter would include the cat and goldfish, because *chattel* in this phrase was once *cattle*, a catch-all for livestock).

Many of the legalistic double-ups are left over from the multilingual nature of England following the Norman Conquest of 1066. The common people spoke English, and the upper crust spoke Norman French, while laws and church matters were in Latin. So many common expressions were rendered in a mixture of English and French (or Latin). *Breaking and entering* is an obvious and well-known example of mixing Old English and French words that mean the same thing.

Legal documents, and to some extent our everyday speech and writing, still bristle with these ageing bilingual barnacles – *last will and testament, bequeath and devise, true and correct, fit and proper, free and clear, save and except, peace and quiet, goods and chattels.*

As David Mellinkoff pointed out in his very readable book *The Language of the Law*, once the doubling became a habit, it was no longer confined to words of different languages. *Let* and *hindrance* are actually both Old English derivatives, with the latter sporting a grafted-on French ending. Other paired Anglo-Saxonisms include *by and with*, to *have and hold*, and *each and every*. And there are some familiar uses of French-only couplets (though there is an obvious Latin influence in some): *aid and abet, rest and residue, cease and desist, authorize and empower, aid and comfort, null and void.*

Not so obvious, perhaps, is the phrase *hue and cry*. The first word has nothing to do with colour, but is from the French *huer*, 'to hoot or cry.' It's only in this redundant phrase that this *hue* is ever used.

In thirteenth-century England and for centuries afterward, the expression described the uproar calling for the pursuit of a felon. Citizens within earshot were legally required both to take up the hue and cry and to join in the chase. Until 1839, *Hue and Cry* was the subtitle of an official gazette of wanted criminals in Britain, and it is still used by the Royal Ulster Constabulary.

That's all well and good, you say, joining in the spirit of things, but doesn't each and every one of us indulge in this hemming and hawing sometimes? And I'd have to say: Yes, examples in common speech are not few and far between, in this day and age.

By hook or by crook, time and tide (as in Yuletide, or season, or time) wait for no one. What with one thing and another, we pick and choose at odds and ends. Remaining outwardly calm, cool, and collected, we struggle with might and main to be fair and square, to tread the straight (once *strait*) and narrow path and avoid rack (read *wrack* or *wreck*) and ruin. But when push comes to shove, and we've looked at all the whys and wherefores, it's best to have a last will and testament (they were once distinct) so that our heirs and successors won't have to slug it out with other kith and kin.

And with that, before somebody smites me hip and thigh, I'd better cease, desist, and sign off.

———————————   •   •   •   ———————————

It is an article of faith, not a matter of fact, that 'posh' derives from 'Port Out, Starboard Home.' The awful, even painful truth is: This theory doesn't hold water.

ALL AT SEA WITH A RED HERRING

HERE'S A LITTLE QUIZ, DESIGNED TO TEST YOUR KNOWLEDGE OF simple – and silly – word origins. There is no prize for the correct answer, but lots of chagrin and mortification for wrong ones. You will have approximately two seconds to come up with your response, and then the rest of the weekend to smash your head against a wall or write me a remonstrative letter.

Ready? Here goes: Of the words *pish, posh, tush, tosh,* and *bosh*, which one derives from an acronym related to sea journeys to and from the East by affluent imperial Britons?

Time's up. The answer is, none of the above. I know a lot of you unhesitatingly chose the second word, because I could hear a chorus of *posh*es pealing from Pugwash to Prince Rupert. Don't feel bad. If you thought *posh* stemmed from an old cruise-ship custom of putting preferred passengers in the 'port-out-starboard-home' cabins, you've got a lot of company. But you, and they, are nevertheless wrong.

Belief in this acronymic but highly apocryphal provenance is one of the most persistent and persuasive fables in the annals of folk etymology. *Posh*, which means 'elegant,' 'exclusive,' and 'expensive,' is listed in most lexicons as 'origin unknown.' It is a rare week in which dictionary editors do not get letters setting them straight on the word's nautical beginnings, often in tones that betray an unmistakable cockiness on the part of the writer for having tumbled to a word origin before the lexicographers did.

Among the myth's adherents and perpetuators was William Manchester, who explained it in his 1983 book *The Last Lion: Winston Spencer Churchill.* The oppressive heat during the Peninsular and Oriental Steam Navigation

Company's four-week voyage to Calcutta 'had become a legend,' Manchester wrote. 'The worst part of the passage was crossing the Red Sea. Those who could afford relative comfort bought ... port-side cabins going out to India and starboard cabins for the trip home; in time, "Port Out, Starboard Home" became the acronym POSH.'

It's just so deucedly neat and fitting, isn't it? The only trouble is, it doesn't hold water. The P & O plied between Britain and its eastern outposts from 1842 to 1970. The earliest appearance of *posh* in print was in *Punch* magazine in 1918. It stretches credulity to the breaking point that such a rippingly splendid adjective would not be seized upon long before then. Perhaps a more telling refutation is that no ticket or other documentation referring to POSH has ever been uncovered by any steamship line. P & O did exploit the legend by using the *posh* poop in advertising during the 1960s.

Like all good myths, this one's had its share of embroidery. According to one elaboration, the initials were stamped on tickets in vivid blue ink. Webster's *Dictionary of Word Origins* recounts the story of an 'eyewitness' who 'saw' the letters stamped on the ticket of a gentleman who had a passage from Australia to England and back. The problem here is that this would have ensured a steamy passage. He would have had the sunny side out and the same going back. Preferential treatment in this case would have demanded the designation SOPH.

The likeliest explanation is that today's *posh* is merely an extended meaning of the nineteenth-century slang word of the same spelling, which meant 'fop' or 'dandy.'

All the other words in our contest list are expressions of contempt or impatience, synonymous with nonsense, rubbish, or balderdash. *Pish, tosh*, and *tush* are naturally occurring ejaculations like *tsk* and *tut*, but in North America *tush* (or the cuter *tushie)* has quite another meaning. Adapted from the Yiddish-American *tuchus* (which in turn is adapted from Hebrew *tahat*, 'beneath'), it means 'backside,' 'buttocks,' or 'anus.'

Bosh came into fashion after it appeared in James J. Morier's *Ayesha, the Maid of Kars* in 1834: 'This firpan [licence or passport] is *bosh* – nothing.' The author borrowed it from the Turkish *bosh*, meaning 'empty' or 'worthless.'

And you can borrow it to use the next time someone tells you about the ocean-going origin of *posh*.

P.S. This column aroused more reader passion than the one a couple of years ago that poked fun at haggis. It called for a more detailed debunking.

All I can say about the reaction is: Gosh! Did I utter a blasphemy or an unspeakable obscenity? Did I step heinously beyond the ever-shifting line of political correctitude? Did I offend the great god Grammaticus by sundering an infinitive, or abuse usage by inferring instead of implying?

No, all I said was pish and tosh to the widely held and obviously cherished belief that *posh* originated as an acronym for 'port out, starboard home.' Among the more moderate reactions to this perceived heresy were two letters to the editor. One was from a 'shattered' David McIntosh, former Ottawa Bureau staffer for Canadian Press. The other, from M. Yvonne Robinson of Etobicoke, adduced the aptly named *Brewer's Dictionary of Phrase and Fable* to bolster her refusal to renounce the highly doubtful derivation of *posh*.

Well, *chacun à son mythe*. If Ms Robinson wants to swear by *Brewer's* 1965 (ninth) edition, that's her business. But she should be aware that the 1989 (fourteenth) edition is slightly but significantly different. Instead of saying *posh* 'has its origin in,' it now reads 'was supposed to have originated in.' And it now ends with the words: 'This traditional explanation is apparently fictitious.'

The word also evaded specialized lexicons for a century, appearing in none of the following dictionaries: Smyth's *Sailor's Word Book* (1867), Ansted's *Dictionary of Sea Terms* (1944), Colcord's *The Sea Language Comes Ashore* (1945), Bradford's *Glossary of Sea Terms* (1927, 1954), Layton's *Dictionary of Nautical Words and Terms* (1955), Burgess's *Dictionary of Sailing* (1961). It turns up in Granville's 1961 *Dictionary of Sailor's Slang*, then soon afterward in Course's 1962 *Dictionary of Nautical Terms*, and, of course, in the 1965 and 1989 *Brewer's*.

Evidence of its use on the P&O – ticket stubs, passenger lists, diaries, anything – has also eluded Lawrence Kimpton, curator of the company's archives in London. According to a note in the January 1971 issue of *The Mariner's Mirror*, Mr Kimpton said the company didn't issue return tickets at the time, so there would be no reference to a return leg on a ticket or anything else, whatever the port of departure.

The author of the note, G. Chowdharay-Best, visited the archives and examined deck plans of ships of the period. He found that in most cases corridors ran between the ships' sides and cabins, so all rooms were out of the direct sun. In addition, while all ships had VIP accommodations, there was no consistency as to which side they were located on. But if they were on the port side going 'out,' they were still on the port side coming 'home.'

It's probable that *posh* is a 'retroactive' acronym – a folk-etymology derivation dreamed up to fit the word. The fact is that acronym-forming was rare until this century. The *Oxford English Dictionary* lists only two for the nineteenth century, and they arose in the 1890s. It's worth noting that, for years, many people swore that the abbreviation for long-johns, 'BVDs' (Bradley, Voorlees, and Day), stood for 'babies' ventilated diapers.'

The word *acronym* itself is only of 1940s vintage, and acronymizing became a virtual fad in the 1960s – about the time that *posh* and its apocryphal etymon began to be noticed by some lexicographers, and swallowed by many people.

———————————   •   •   •   ———————————

The fact that many neutral words once associated with rural people now have become epithets proves that bad often triumphs over good – at least in semantic affairs.

ARE PHILLIES FANS 'BOORS' OR WORSE?

I N A STORY ABOUT PHILADELPHIA PHILLIES PITCHER MITCH 'WILD Thing' Williams, hapless scapegoat of the 1993 World Series, the *Globe* sports section described the behaviour of some decidedly disgruntled Philly fans as 'boorish.'

This 'boorish' behaviour involved smashing windows and throwing eggs and paint at Williams's home, and, oh yes, threatening his life. This leaves us with two semantic possibilities: a) standards of etiquette have sunk so low in Philadelphia that violently antisocial activities are considered merely rude, like forgetting to say 'sorry' after shooting someone for cutting in front of you in the cafeteria queue; or b) the word *boor* has skidded pretty well to the very bottom of the slippery slope of pejoration – a fall from grace that began many centuries ago.

The Anglo-Saxon word for a dwelling or cottage was *bur*, and the occupant was a *gebur*, 'a dweller, farmer, or countryman.' Someone who dwelt just down the road was *neah-gebur*, or 'near-dweller,' from which we derived *neighbour*. In East Anglia, where many archaisms are lovingly or unknowingly preserved, people still familiarly call a neighbour 'bor.'

By Shakespeare's time, *boor* was a common English word for 'farmer' – an association that virtually guaranteed its semantic degeneration. Supercilious city-folk have turned many neutral words for country cousins into epithets – including *villain* (originally a feudal serf, from Latin *villa*, 'country house') and *churl* (from Old English *ceorl*, 'serf'), not to mention *farmer* and *peasant* themselves.

It's common for pejorative senses of words to eclipse other meanings, and by the nineteenth century, *boor* was rarely if ever used without a contemptuous connotation. The triumph of bad over good was authenticated by explorer David Livingstone, in his book *Missionary Travels and Researches in South Africa* (1857). 'The word *Boer*,' he explained, 'simply means "farmer", and is not synonymous with our word *boor*.' Indeed, by this time *boor* had shed its rustic associations and was used to describe any ill-mannered jerk.

Members of this prolific Germanic word-family were evolving in Europe too, eventually producing the modern German *Bauer* and modern Dutch *boer*, both meaning 'farmer or peasant.' The former has a capital *b* because all German nouns do, and the latter acquired one when it came to mean specifically Dutch settlers in South Africa in the early nineteenth century. German also has *Nachbar*, and Dutch has *buurman*, for 'neighbour.'

Another word in the same boorish ballpark, or back forty, is *bumpkin*, which has three possible derivations. The simplest is that it's a diminutive of *bum*, as in 'buttocks.' The second is that it comes from a Middle Dutch word *bommekijn*, or 'little barrel.' The fact that early contexts suggest a short, stumpy man lends credence to that speculation. The third theory is that *bumpkin* was adapted from the Dutch *boomken*, or 'little tree,' again with the suggestion of stocky loutishness. The Dutch and German words for tree, *boom* and *Baum*, sprouted from an Indo-European root meaning 'growing thing.' It was from that same root, growing in another direction, that we derived that Old English *bur*, 'cottage,' and its offspring *boor* and *neighbour*.

It also led to *bower*, a variant of *bur*. For some reason this word caught on with the poets, who idealized it first as a rustic cottage, then a bedchamber, a lady's boudoir, and finally an idyllic tree-shaded place. Another kind of *bower*, influenced by the German *Bauer*, was a servant boy, or *knave*, a word that has also suffered from severe pejoration. The only survivors of this sense are the *bowers*, or 'knaves,' in a deck of playing-cards.

A closely related Dutch word, *bouwerij*, a 'farm, plantation, or estate,' produced an English word with anything but idyllic overtones. One of New York's most famous colonists, Peter Stuyvesant, had an estate in lower Manhattan. A street was named for it, and eventually the area took on the street's name. It was the Bowery, which became a neighbourhood of saloons, flophouses, and human derelicts, and a synonym for urban squalor.

In my youth, a popular matinee movie series featured a tough gang known as the Bowery Boys. Judging by recent reports, they've moved to the City of Brotherly Love.

———————————   •   •   •   ———————————

Sew, a needle sewing thread. Seam, a word that follows sew. Steamy, a drink with jam and bread, which brings us back to squalid and sordid erotica. Everybody sing!

WHY SEAMY IS JUST NOT SEEMLY

A RECENT ISSUE OF THE MAGAZINE *ARCHAEOLOGY* MADE PASSING reference to a book collection of 'seamy erotica.' When Robert Ackman of Dartmouth, Nova Scotia, saw this, he first thought it was a typo – that someone had not only forgotten to cross the *t* but neglected to put it in in the first place. 'Then I recollected that *seamy* has been applied to the "seamy side of town",' Mr Ackman wrote, 'and I wondered at the derivation in that context.'

Seamy is indeed what it seems, an adjective for the noun *seam*, as in the junction of two pieces of cloth, sewn together. *Seam* is one of those down-to-earth, venerable English words that are spelled the same today as they were more than a thousand years ago. It is related to *sew*, which is thousands of years older, rooted in the Indo-European *syu*, to 'bind or stitch.' So *sew* and *seam*, so it seems, go naturally together.

That's straightforward enough, but how did *seamy* develop into a word that gives erotica a bad name? Centrefold playmates, I'm told, have staples and fold-creases, but no seams. The answer lies, like so many answers, in Shakespeare.

The earliest known written use of *seamy* is in Othello (1604) when Emilia says to Iago: 'Some such squire he was / That turn'd your wit the seamy side without / And made you to suspect me with the Moor.' Since wits don't have seams any more than nudie photos do, this was not only the first recorded use of the adjective, but also the first figurative use. In the context, it meant either 'coarse,' as the rough side of a seam, or 'inside-out,' i.e., opposite to what is usual.

Though *seamy* was used occasionally in a literal sense in the eighteenth and nineteenth centuries, Shakespeare's metaphorical 'seamy side' really caught on. By the mid-1800s it had degenerated from coarse to downright disagreeable. In his *History of Frederick the Great* (1865), Thomas Carlyle wrote of 'the splendid and the sordid, the seamy side and the smooth, of life at Cirey.'

To achieve synonymity with *sordid* is about as low as a word can go. In Latin, *sordidus* meant 'dirty, foul, base, and mean.' In English, *sordid* was at first (around 1600) a medical term describing a festering, pustular sore – a word to which, oddly enough, it is unrelated.

Like many medical and other scientific and technical terms, *sordid* was soon appropriated by the masses, and applied to anybody or anything foul, filthy, repellant, and squalid. Later, it more often described personal character, marked by ignoble, selfish, or mercenary tendencies. Henry Cardinal Manning, archbishop of Westminster, thought these were pretty widespread characteristics when he wrote in 1875: 'All men of the world are sordid, and the more worldly, the more sordid.'

Squalid is another word that's unmistakably on the seamy side of our vocabulary. Robert Burton, in his brilliant survey of Elizabethan beliefs and behaviour, *Anatomy of Melancholy* (1621), defined it as well as any subsequent dictionary: 'What can poverty give else, but beggary, fulsome nastiness, squalor ... drudgery, labour, ugliness?'

The Latin parent *squalidus* meant 'dry, scabby, and dirty.' When the word came into English in the late sixteenth century, it carried this physical denotation, but also conveyed a sense of mental agony, misery, and wretchedness.

Wretch is the most etymologically fascinating in this woeful list. In Old English the word was *wrecca*, in Old High German *reccho*, and they both signified 'exile.' The Anglo-Saxon exile brooded over his banishment, becoming deeply nostalgic and morose, and ending up as a poor, often contemptible *wretch*. The German exile, however, made the best of a bad situation, becoming first an adventurer, then a knight errant, and finally, as *Recke* in Modern German, a noble warrior or hero – a remarkable contrast to the English sense development.

And that, seamingly, is all the misery and degradation we can handle this week – and probably a lot more than Mr Ackman bargained for.

•   •   •

A great many English words have a history of numerals in their development. For a change of pace, here's a little quiz that challenges you to find some well-disguised numbers.

WRITING BY NUMBERS

It was a dark and stormy September afternoon. Dean Smith's deadline loomed only hours away, and every second counted. There was something I couldn't put my finger on, so I paced the floor, side to side and kitty-corner, hoping physical exertion would help me sift out the trivia and fathom the true dimensions of my quandary. I needed some high-octane ideas soon, or my number would be up.

THAT PSEUDO-GOTHIC GABBLE IS A MYSTERY IN ITSELF. IN addition to the words *counted*, *one*, and *number*, it contains words or word parts with numerical connections from one to ten. How many can you decipher (Another one! – from the Arabic *sifr*, or 'zero') before I go ahead and spill the beans?

1. Did you skim right over *only*? This inconspicious but much-used adjective starts us at square one. In fact, it's merely *one* with the *e* removed and the modifying *-ly* tacked on.

2. The second answer is *second*. But wait a minute – how did this adjective become a noun meaning a tiny bit of time? It's really short for what the ancients called *pars minuta secunda*, or 'second small part.' The *pars minuta prima*, or 'first small part' (one-sixtieth of an hour), is what we call a minute.

3. The intersection of three roads, in Latin *tri via*, was a place where travellers met and exchanged small talk while they rested. So *trivia* has come to mean insignificant things, except to the inventors of Trivial Pursuit.

4. *Kitty-corner* is a cutie. It's a mongrelized version of *cater-corner*, the first element of which has been popularly confused with the feline *cater* in

caterwaul and *caterpillar* (hairy cat). But this *cater* comes from the French *quatre*, 'four.' *Quandary*, which looks as though it could have a four somewhere in its family tree, is a red herring. Its origin is unknown.

5. Thumbs up and a high five to you if you singled out *finger*. It's from an ancient Indo-European word *penkweros*, which became the Germanic *fingwraz*, or 'one of five.'

6. A *fathom* is a measure of six feet. But why? Probably first used by an angler describing the one that got away, it comes from an Old Saxon word *fathmos*, meaning 'both arms outstretched.'

7. *September* is an easy one. From the Latin *septem*, 'seven,' it denoted the seventh month of the year in the Roman calendar. The educationist Pope Gregory XIII, anticipating New Math by about four centuries, made it the ninth month in his new calendar, the one commonly used today.

8. Here's one for the chemistry crowd. *Octane* is a paraffin made up of eight parts carbon and eighteen parts hydrogen. The figurative expression *high-octane*, meaning 'energetic' or 'potent,' is an erroneous interpretation of 'high octane number,' which relates not to power but to the anti-knock properties of petroleum fuel.

9. This one's hidden on the back-side of *afternoon*. *Noon* comes from the Latin *nona*, 'ninth,' and originally signified the ninth hour after sunrise, or around 3 p.m. Also known as *nones* in church circles, it was gradually appropriated by the laity, and by the fourteenth century was understood to mean 'midday.' No one seems to know why, but we can't pin this time-switch on Gregory, who wasn't yet born.

10. If you spotted *dean* as the last digital datum in our mystery, you're on the honours list. It's from the Latin *decanus*, a military term for the commander of a division of ten men. By the fifth century it referred to the head of ten monks in a monastery, but the numerical signification became fuzzy by the fourteenth century, when the label was applied to Oxford and Cambridge fellows whose job was to maintain discipline among various numbers of subordinates and students.

We still have *deans* in academe, but the word also broadly denotes the senior member of a peer group. For the latter, some people prefer the fancy French cousin, *doyen*. *Deacon*, which more closely resembles *decanus*, does not derive from it; it's from the Greek word for 'servant,' *diakonos* (literally, 'thoroughly active one').

To sum up: Figures don't lie, as the expression goes, but some odd numerals – and even ones too – lie behind a great number of English words and phrases.

_____ • • • _____

The old pedagogic symbol for 'and' was once pronounced 'and-pussy-and' – & for reasons that should be purr-fectly clear.

X, Y, Z & THEN THERE'S ONE MORE

R ECENTLY RAMBLING IN PURSUIT OF BIBLICAL WORD ODDITIES, I stumbled on one of those statistical curiosities that are at the same time stupefyingly inconsequential and inescapably fascinating. According to Cobham Brewer's *Dictionary of Phrase and Fable* (1894 edition), the word *and* appears in the Bible 44,227 times.

Just think about it. Enough *ands* to fill a two-hundred-page paperback. Eight times more *ands* than the combined populations of Andréville, Quebec, Anderdon, Ontario, and Andrew, Alberta. So many *ands* that if you placed them *and-to-and* they would stretch for more than two kilometres (in twelve-point Times Roman) and still never reach a conclusion.

It's little wonder that old-fashioned word-processors – i.e., human persons with quill pens and inkhorns, to whom cursors were messengers and icons were pictures of saints – needed an abbreviation for the ubiquitous conjunction, short as it already was. They found it in the curlicued character &, which at first was not an abbreviation at all, but a cursive form of *et*, Latin for 'and.'

The symbol was part of the *Notae Tironianae*, or Tironian Notes, one of the earliest shorthand systems. It was invented in 63 BC by Marcus Tullius Tiro, a scholarly freed slave who did secretarial work for the statesman-orator Cicero. Tiro published a shorthand dictionary that helped the emperors Titus and Julius Caesar write their speeches, memos, and memoirs, and was widely used by church scribes throughout Europe for more than one thousand years.

The dawn of the Middle Ages was the sunset for Tiro's system, however, as shorthand – along with many other creative but not widely understood things – became associated with magic and witchcraft and fell into disrepute and, inevitably, disuse.

Even curiouser than the symbol itself is the English word that eventually came to stand for &. The word is *ampersand*, which, with three times as many letters and syllables as the word it purports to truncate, seems to defeat the purpose.

If one didn't have recourse to stacks of etymological resources, one might be tempted to surmise that *ampersand* has something to do with electrical currents on the beach. One would still be sorely challenged to make a connection with the common word *and*, but it's no wilder a speculation than one theory that was given some credence in the nineteenth century.

According to this whimsical wordlore, the word was originally *and-pussy-and*. This made perfect sense to its proponents, who pointed out that & looks just like a cat sitting up with one forepaw extended. In fact, the word was at times spelt *ampusand* and *ampussyand*, but it's not certain whether these corruptions preceded or resulted from the outlandish feline folk etymology.

Some people argued the spurious *ampusand* came closer to the pronunciation of the original phrase than the accepted modern one. Nevertheless, harrumphed etymologist Walter Skeat in an 1871 article in *Notes and Queries*, 'it does not follow that it is therefore derived from a pussy-cat.'

The real story is just as odd, if somewhat less charming. Several centuries ago English schoolchildren learning the alphabet had to distinguish between the letter *a* and the indefinite article 'a.' They did this by describing the latter as *a per se a*. The *per se* is Latin for 'by itself,' and the oft-repeated classroom phrase meant '*a* by itself makes the word *a*.' The pronoun 'I' got similar treatment.

Similarly, they learned the meaning of the common & by reciting *and per se and*, which meant in full, 'the character & by itself represents the word *and*.' So normal was the use of the symbol in writing that it regularly appeared as a twenty-seventh member of the alphabet in early 'ABC' books. Classroom recitations of the alphabet ended with 'X, Y, Zed and *and per se and*.' A slurred pronunciation of this eventually yielded the modern spelling *ampersand*.

Use of the ampersand with the Latin *cetera* (the rest), or just with the letter *c*, became popular in the fifteenth century. Later it caught on as a short-cut for those flowery and fulsome sign-offs at the end of letters. Instead of writing, 'I beg to remain, Sir, your most obliging and respectful servant,' correspondents saved a lot of ink with a terse and economic 'Yrs &c.'

———————————   •   •   •   ———————————

What is it about words that end in '-ard' that make them so vituperative? It started as a German suffix meaning 'hardy' but the French and Dutch made a mockery of it.

'ARD LINES

'MAYBE I'M A DULLARD, BUT ...' THE LETTER-TO-THE-EDITOR writer began, then with nimble argument demonstrated that he wasn't. I was induced to read his epistle, not so much by the trusty rhetorical approach as by that fusty word *dullard*. It seemed to carry a thin, fuzzy coating of mildew, as if summoned for this rare duty from the attic of obsolescence.

It got me thinking about other words that end in *-ard*, a process that inevitably involved hours delving in dictionaries. Unaided, I could conjure up only ten, not counting *blackguard* and *blowhard*, which, while conforming to the pejorative pattern of the *-ard* words, were not formed as the others by the simple suffixal addition. My list, after *dullard*, counted *dotard, bastard, buzzard, coward, dastard, drunkard, laggard, lollard, niggard,* and *wizard.* Of those, only the last would be taken today with equanimity, although *wizard* wasn't always complimentary. The delightful and certainly disparaging *canard* also occurred to me, but I had already decided to limit my search to personal epithets.

And what a rich lode of dormant invective I tapped! The *OED2* lists about five dozen *-ard* words to describe people of unsavoury character or underdeveloped intellect, and all but the handful above now languish in dusty disuse. Virtually all of them are derogatory, and some of them are so mordantly mean that I can only lament their loss – perhaps to a precursor wave of today's political correctitude? The next question was this: What was it about *-ard* that appealed to our bad-mouthing forebears?

Some time between the eighth and twelfth centuries, German-speakers began honouring heroes and other eminences by adding *-hart* or *-hard* to their names, to denote 'hardy.' The practice carried over into Middle High German and Dutch, where it developed a sarcastic edge and became generally derisive. The French adopted the habit as an intensifier of masculine nouns, proper and improper, and this too became mostly pejorative, as in *vieillard*, 'old fool,' *mouchard*, 'sneak' or 'informer' (from *mouche*, 'fly'), and *froussard*, 'coward' (from *frousse*, 'fright'). It travelled to England, as did many things French, after the Norman Conquest. At first the English were content with unalloyed borrowings, but then began tacking the invidious *-ard* onto purely English words, thus producing the likes of *drunkard*, *laggard*, and *sluggard*.

Before long, there were many, both imported and home-grown. They fell into three main categories: words for fools, idlers, and wastrels; for people with other undesirable or downright antisocial attributes; and for those with some physical shortcoming.

In the first category were *babelard* or *babillard* for 'babbler'; *lubbard* for 'big, stupid lout' (from which came *landlubber*); *caynard*, 'lazy dog' (ultimately from the Italian *cagna*, 'bitch'); *losard*, 'rake,' 'profligate' (from Old English *losel*, 'one who is lost to perdition'); and the mellifluous but contumelious *musard*, whose sin was day-dreaming.

Even more to be censured were the peevish and fretful *fretchards*, the penny-pinching *misards* and *muglards*, the parasitic, hypocritical sycophants known as *papelards* (after Italian *pappalardo*, 'one who eats bacon fat'), the pilfering *pillards*, the puling, pusillanimous *snivelards*, the deceitful *trichards* (after Old French *trichart*, 'tricker'), and the loathsome loners called *unkards* (a dialect word related to *awkward*).

More to be pitied than censured, but censured nonetheless, were citizens who fell short of physical perfection. They included the scantily coifed *ballard*, and squinting, weak-eyed *blincard* (who could also be one who deliberately ignored reality), the hobbling mendicant *clochard* (from French *clocher*, 'to limp') or *limpard*, the stammering *mafflard*, and the *scallards* and *scabbards* who suffered from some skin disease.

A subspecies of *-ard* word, if not of humans, might be labelled 'political.' In this charming group we find *Dynamitard*, an explosive nineteenth-century French radical leftist; *Dreyfusard*, erstwhile bleeding-heart supporter of Capt. Alfred Dreyfus, wrongly convicted of treason in 1894 and exonerated in 1906; *Cagoulard* (from French 'wearer of a monk's cowl'), a member of a sort of 1930s French Ku Klux Klan; and *Communard*, an adherent of the Commune of Paris, a group that took over the municipal government of the

French capital and played a leading role in the post-revolutionary Reign of Terror. Members of a sixteenth-century faction were called *Guisards*, a name that conveniently blended their loyalty to the Duc de Guise and their penchant for wearing extravagant costumes.

Guisard was also used extensively in Scotland and northern England as a variant of *guiser*, a 'mummer.' A dialect pronunciation of the latter probably yielded the word *geezer*, slang for an 'old man.'

This by no means exhausts the store of sleeping slurs that once formed an 'ard core of popular insult. Some seem definitely to deserve rehabilitation, but with others that would be nothing but foolhardy.

———————————   •   •   •   ———————————

WHAT'S THE USAGE?

The popularity of new words and phrases could no longer skyrocket if the movement spearheaded by these sticks-in-the-mud ever trickled down to the masses.

LANGUAGE SAVIOURS ARE DEAD(LY) SERIOUS

I F I EVER WRITE A BOOK ABOUT MY RELATIONSHIP WITH THE language, I'll be tempted to call it 'Dr Strangelingo, or How I Learned to Stop Worrying and Love the Abominations.'

People often ask me if I have a pet language peeve, and they're usually disappointed to hear that I don't. Others seem anxious to hear my assessment of our language's health, their rhetorical questions leaving no doubt about their own pessimism. They too are crestfallen – and sometimes even a mite testy – when I opine that English is as robust as it ever was, and probably more so.

'What about using nouns as verbs?' they probe (using a noun that got verbed in the seventeenth century). My reply – that we made verbs from nouns before we made arrowheads from flint, and have continued, fortunately, to do so – usually leaves them anguished (noun-to-verb, fourteenth century).

I could advise them, I suppose, to send their axes to be ground by the public relations staff at Lake Superior State University in Sault Ste Marie, Michigan. Each year in January, these well-meaning but misguided people issue a 'List of Words Banished from the Queen's English for Mis-Use, Over-Use or General Uselessness.'

Obviously oblivious of King Canute's demonstration of the impossibility of stemming the tide, and perhaps ignorant of Samuel Johnson's warning of the futility of trying to 'lash the wind,' these self-appointed sentinels purport to proscribe words and phrases that have been sent in by puritanical finger-pointers, many of them from Canada. What's worse, their proclamations are eagerly awaited by the news media, slavishly published in the same tone of reverence used for the equally irrelevant 'best-dressed' lists, and often heralded by hand-wringing editorials.

Even conceding that some neologisms and phrases become irksomely fashionable, and conceding that *offload* may be superfluous, why banish the words? Isn't that like putting all the matches in jail and letting the pyromaniacs run free?

Like most crusaders, the PR people at LSSU allow their cause to cloud their reason. On this year's 'Banished in Perpetuity' list is *dead serious*, nominated for exile by Caleb Hartmann of St Mary's Cathedral High School in Gaylord, Michigan, who commented: 'While death is certainly a serious business, if you are dead you certainly won't be able to convince people how serious you are.'

Mr Hartmann is not only dead wrong but also dead serious from the neck up. The figurative use of the adjective *dead*, to mean 'quite,' 'absolutely,' or 'utterly,' has been around for more than four centuries. It's widely used in many other metaphorical senses – dead to the world, dead on one's feet, on the dead run, in the dead of night – some dating back to the Middle Ages. Would Caleb Hartmann and LSSU throw these on the scrap heap too? Probably not; in their ultra-literal world, you can't 'throw' phrases, and there's no scrap heap nearby.

Larry Hogue of Corpus Christi, Texas, says *skyrocket* and *spearhead* 'are non-verbs which should be tossed onto the junk heap.' Why? Every dictionary on the market today accepts both of these highly descriptive action words as verbs. Who is Larry Hogue to say nay, and who are the arbiters at LSSU to agree? Okay, some writers overuse them; if so, it's the writers, not the words, that should be trashed (a noun only recently verbified).

The LSSU gurus have been gleefully word-whacking since 1976. Here are some other useful words and expressions they have unsuccessfully 'banished' over the years: *microwaveable* (what could be clearer or shorter?); *fun*, as an adjective (ditto); *trickle-down effect* (dripping with expressive meaning); *fax*, as a verb (how about *phone, telex, wire, cable, telegraph*? Ban them too?); *user-friendly* (one of many useful coinages from the computer world); *grandfather*, as a verb (a natural extension of the imaginative 'grandfather clause'); *deplane* (you'd rather have *unplane, off-plane, disembark*?); *prioritize* (perfectly standard verbification; it means more than *rank*, which is also a verbified noun).

'The language most likely to continue long without alteration,' wrote Dr Johnson in the celebrated preface to his dictionary, 'would be that of a nation raised a little, and but a little, above barbarity.'

Thus, LSSU prefers the fancy phrase *banished in perpetuity* over the older, shorter, and plainer *banned forever*, which really boils down (that's a figure of speech, Caleb) to the same thing.

———————————   •   •   •   ———————————

Like a lot of words, 'alternative' has evolved in meaning over the years. But there are still some purists who insist that it should mean what it used to – nothing more, nothing less.

'ALTERNATIVE' IS A CHOICE WORD

A RECENT LETTERS-TO-THE-EDITOR SKIRMISH OVER THE MEANING of the expression 'alternative lifestyle' coincided with the arrival of two missives to this corner, taking issue with an alleged misuse of the noun *alternative*.

The first quarrel involved the 'Alternative Lifestyles' heading in the *Globe and Mail*'s 'Voice Personals' page, a sort of telephonic lonely-hearts column. A reader claimed the heading really meant 'same-sex relationships' or 'gay/ lesbian ads,' and that the *Globe* should come right out and say so. A second reader accused the first of paranoia, and said 'Alternative Lifestyles' was plain enough English for homosexual match-ups.

This letters-page logomachy is part of a fairly new controversy over the meaning of *alternative*. The cavils aimed at 'Word Play' were based on a much older disputation. At issue was a column about the word *genuine* in current General Motors advertising of 'Genuine Chevrolet' (see page 87). It was suggested that while GM had 'plenty of alternatives,' it chose *genuine* because it was mellifluous, if meaningless.

Both correspondents applauded this observation but pounced on 'plenty of alternatives.' One raised a 'small objection,' and the other was 'shocked' that I would even hint at the possibility of more than two alternatives to anything. 'Even in this age of sloppy use of the Queen's English,' said Mr Shocked, 'there can surely be only two alternatives altogether or, more precisely, one alternative to any given item.'

Here's another shock: This 'sloppy' use of the Queen's English was going on when the queen was Victoria. One of the slobs was William Gladstone, who wrote in 1857: 'When in doubt among several alternatives of conduct, we are bound to choose that which has the greatest likelihood of being right.'

Another, among many others, was John Stuart Mill (1848): 'The alternative seemed to be either death, or to be permanently supported by other people, or a radical change in the economical arrangements.'

In fact, the use was slipping into the language more than a century before that. The 1753 Supplement to *Chambers Cyclopoedia* defined the legal term *alternative promise* as a condition in which 'two or more are engaged to do a thing.'

Yet the either/or 'rule' persists among purists, because the word derives from the Latin *alter*, 'the other of two,' or 'the second.' But when we're not in Rome, we're not obliged to do as the Romans do. If we were, the simple verb *arrive* would still mean 'to land on a riverbank,' and *nausea* would mean only seasickness.

My surprised correspondent might be even more stunned to know that even his narrow definition was considered slipshod a century and a half ago. *Alternative*, insisted Edward Gould in *Good English* (1867), 'means a choice – *one* choice – between two things. Yet popular usage has so corrupted it, that it is now commonly applied to the things themselves, and not to the choice between them. And, indeed, some people go so far as to say "*several* alternatives were presented to him." '

Gould's anguish indicates that popular usage had won the day by the year of Canada's birth as a nation. That it still shocks people is – well – stupefying.

An even older cause of fretfulness is the confusion of the adjectives *alternative* (other) and *alternate* (occurring one after the other, in turns). Most dictionaries and usage authorities, such as the *Globe and Mail Style Book*, uphold the distinction, but concede to usage the ingrained political term *alternate delegate*, where the adjective means exactly the same thing as *alternative*.

The newer dispute began in the 1960s, when such labels as alternative society, medicine, press, energy, and other things sprang up. They often carried a political, anti-establishment connotation which guaranteed semantic debate such as in the recent letters to the editor.

Maybe we should all just calm down, and get a life. Or, alternatively, a lifestyle. Or even an alternative lifestyle.

———————————   •   •   •   ———————————

'Presently' is one of those words that are a pettifogger's pet – or bête noire – but what does it really mean? That depends on where you are, and maybe on how much time you've got.

ITS PAST IS VARIED, ITS PRESENT CONFUSED

THERE IS NO TIME LIKE THE PRESENT – OR VERY SOON HEREAFTER – for dealing with the nettlesome word *presently* and some of its fellow-travellers. This prosaic word has the volatile capacity to send normally placid people into paroxysms of frustrated rage. As soon as they hear it 'misused' they start twitching. Directly, their eyeballs dilate. Forthwith, smoke can be seen emanating from their ears. By and by, they calm down, and anon, their lives go on – for the present.

Presently is one of a handful of what could be called defining words – acid tests used by pedants to identify peasants. For a while, *hopefully* performed the same taxonomic role for pettifoggers who would not think twice about using other sentence-starting adverbs, such as *clearly, fortunately, frankly,* or *interestingly*.

So what does *presently* mean? We'll get to that straightaway, but first let's look at *presently*'s past. The adjective *present* was borrowed from the French in the fourteenth century and meant 'here,' or the opposite of 'absent.' The earliest meaning of the adverb *presently* was 'in person.' This sense lasted only about two hundred years, during which two other, time-related senses developed.

One was 'at present,' 'currently,' or 'now.' For reasons unclear, this use all but disappeared from English literature during the seventeenth century, but continued in most English dialects, and never went out of style in Scotland and North America. It's back in common use in England, and in Canada today it's virtually the only sense. In virtually all newspaper uses, their style-book proscriptions notwithstanding, it means 'at present,' and in most cases could be replaced by 'now.'

The other main sense was 'at once' or 'right this minute.' When Proteus, one of Shakespeare's *Two Gentlemen of Verona*, told Julia to 'go presently, and take this ring with thee,' he meant pronto.

But then, as now, when people said 'right away' they didn't always mean instantly. By the seventeenth century, *presently* had lost its immediacy, at least in literary English, and came to mean only 'in a little while' or 'shortly.' This is the meaning to which the fussbudgets cling, despite the fact that it is a weak, imprecise, and illogical corruption of the original word.

The human tendency to postpone has sapped other similar words of their urgency. The Old English word *sona*, which would become our *soon*, conveyed a no-nonsense 'without delay.' So clear was this meaning that the word had no comparative or superlative forms. You couldn't be more or most 'immediately.' By the Middle Ages, however, people had caught on that when they heard a taped message saying, 'please stay on the line; a service person will be with you soon,' a longish wait was probably in store. So sooner became later.

The adverb *directly* also suffered from this natural dilatoriness. It originally meant 'immediately,' then 'as soon as,' and now can be taken as 'after a while.' Same with *straightaway*. *By-and-by* once meant 'directly,' and has weakened to 'some time or other.'

Anon, scarcely found outside of poetry or in the stock phrase *ever and anon*, once meant 'instantly.' This word has not only been blunted by time, it's been turned upside down. In Old English it was *on an*, or 'in one,' and was an elliptical short form of 'in a single motion' or 'in one moment.'

In the King James Bible (1611), St Matthew tells the parable of the sower, part of which reads: 'But he that receiveth the seed into stony places, the same is he that receiveth the word, and anon with joy receiveth it.' That *anon* meant immediately, but a reader today might well think there was some interval between the reception of the word and the resulting exultation.

Forthwith seems to have kept its crispness, but is rarely used, except, I understand, in some law books, where it means 'within twenty-four hours.' *Immediately* still means what it says, and *now* is fairly unambiguous, although the fact that it sometimes needs strengthening with the intensifiers *even*, *just*, and *right* might cause concern for its health.

Procrastination may be the thief of time, as the adage says, but it can also mug word meanings.

———————————   •   •   •   ———————————

There are only a few examples of the English subjunctive still breathing, as it were. The trouble is, they seem to generate a lot of growls from self-appointed watchdogs of the language.

IN THE MOOD FOR A SUBJUNCTIVE

FAR BE IT FROM ME TO SPOIL GOOD, CLEAN PECKSNIFFIAN FUN BY pooh-poohing efforts to preserve the subjunctive mood. Heaven forbid! Suffice it to say that, were I in a satirical mood, I would pillory these puritanical pedantries, come what may.

As it is, the above paragraph contains just about all the subjunctivity (and alliteration) you'll ever need. It encompasses nearly all there is left of this grammatical dinosaur.

But there are those who will not let the beast die a dignified, humane, and much-deserved death. A Vancouver letter-to-the-editor writer shed crocodile tears over a *Globe and Mail* headline that read, 'Major wishes his role was minor.' A would-be guru in another newspaper waxed wroth over the 'illiteracy' of a playwright who was quoted in the *Globe* as uttering, 'If I wasn't creative, I would be crazy.' In both cases, the writers insisted the verb should have been the subjunctive *were*.

If my hunch be right, it were fruitless to try to persuade these wilful watchdogs they're barking up the wrong birch. Except for a few fossilized formulas – far be it, as it were, suffice it to say, if I (you, he, she, it) were, if need be, come the revolution, God Save the King's English! – the subjunctive mood is toast, or at best stale bread.

I doubt that these self-appointed preservationists would say or write 'if my hunch be right' or 'it were fruitless' – both legitimate but long-fallow uses of the subjunctive. I suspect their solicitude is selective, and that they not only break their own 'rule' every day, but also use subjunctives they're not even aware of (such as the conjunction *albeit*, a contraction of *all though it be*).

Traditionally, English verbs came in three states of mind, or moods (or modes, as they were once more logically known): the garden variety indicative (I am asking you to leave); the insistent imperative (gedoudahere!); and the irresolute subjunctive (Were you to absent yourself, I should be immensely gratified). Other moods, such as jocular, irritable, contemplative, and funky, have not gained official recognition among grammarians.

Subjunctive describes being subjoined, or dependent. It has also been labelled the 'potential' or 'optative' mood. It was used in sentences involving something contingent, conditional, hypothetical, prospective, conceivable, or wished-for.

It fell into three categories. One was 'mandative,' expressing an order, request, or recommendation, and following such phrases as *it is necessary that*. Examples: it's essential that you be on time; I move the meeting be adjourned; she recommended that he seek help. This form had an elegant simplicity, in that it always used the bare-bones form of the verb, straight from the infinitive, be it in the first, second, or third person, singular or plural. Conjugational bliss, as it were. Mandative subjunctives now are often replaced by the simple indicative (... essential that you are on time) or a *should* contrivance (... recommended that he should seek help).

The second category was of the 'if need be' formulaic sort mentioned above.

The third was the conditional or hypothetical variety, the cause of much grief and controversy. Here is where the 'past' subjunctive *were* gets into the act, to express wishes or conditions contrary to fact (If I were a rich man ...). The damnable thing about it is that, even though it's a past tense form, it's only used to describe the present and future. Go figure.

Confusion over this often causes English speakers to do two things. One is to 'hyper-correct' (*She asked me if I were ticklish*; this should be the simple past indicative *was*). The other is to use the indicative *was* instead of 'correct' *were*, as the wicked *Globe* did – and as respectable writers such as Marlowe, Defoe, Swift, Addison, Byron, Thackeray, Frost, Lamb, Carroll, and Chomsky have been doing since the sixteenth century, without losing a micron of meaning.

Be that as it may, reader Walter Prendergast thinks the subjunctive still has a future. He has an 1886 edition of the *Ontario Public School Grammar*, which describes it as a mood of 'doubtful assertion.' This, he maintains, assures its survival, 'because our politicians use it all day, every day.' Amen, and so be it.

———————————————   •   •   •   ———————————————

It's hardly surprising that a lot of people confuse words that look and sound alike and have similar meanings. 'Furor' and 'furore,' for instance, have a common Latin root.

IF YOU'VE GOT IT, FLAUNT/FLOUT IT

A LOT OF FOLKS ARE IN A FUROR/FURORE OVER THE APPARENTLY increasing misuse of such look-alikes as flaunt/flout, and they often write letters asking if there is any way to stanch/staunch the flow of these abuses of the language.

The short answer is no. The longer one is that these are only a few of the tens of thousands of English words that are undergoing change even as we speak, write, or otherwise employ language to express thought. Furor is futile, and furore is uncalled for. The blurring of meaning in these pairs stems not only from their orthographic, semantic, and phonetic similarity, but also from the fact that they were the same words to begin with.

Furor and *furore* both come from the Latin *furere*, 'to rage or be insane.' The shorter word entered English in the fifteenth century, denoting fury, wrath, or madness. Later its meaning broadened to include the inspired frenzy of poets and prophets, and later still it came to signify great enthusiasm or excitement – a fad or 'rage.'

Meanwhile the Italian version, *furore*, had developed to precisely the same point. Some English writers in the late eighteenth century decided to import the Italian word to distinguish the newer, more positive meaning from the original one. *Furore* would be the uproarious cheering of, say, an adoring opera audience; *furor* would cover the rabid bawling of a riotous mob.

It was a slight distinction, and it was doomed from the start. The two have been used interchangeably ever since the arrival of the second, although the angry sense now prevails in both.

The sticklers' stand on *stanch* and *staunch* is that the former is always a verb, meaning 'to stop the flow of something,' and the latter is always an adjective, meaning 'loyal, principled, and resolute.' While most dictionaries lean toward this differentiation, all of them list the words as variants of each other – reluctant acknowledgment of the interchangeable role they have played for about six hundred years.

They're both rooted in Latin, but even in this there's controversy. Some scholars say the forerunner is *stancare*, a contraction of *stagnicare*, which also produced the Modern English *stagnate*. Others feel the source is *stanticare*, a Vulgar Latin version of *stare*, 'to stand.' Maybe the Romans quarrelled as much over that as we do over *stanch* and *staunch*.

It may surprise the sticklers that the earliest *stanch/staunch* was not only a verb and adjective, but also a noun, meaning anything used to stop the flow of blood. As a verb it also meant to 'quench thirst' or 'satisfy hunger.' The Scots muddied things further by spelling it *stench(e)* and using it as a synonym for 'quell' or 'suppress.'

As an adjective, the word had an equally acute identity crisis. Originally spelled *stawnche*, it meant 'watertight.' Since a *stawnche* ship was a good ship, the modifier came to mean 'strong' or 'solid.' Later it was applied to people who were highly principled and loyal. Sir Walter Scott even used it to describe the qualities themselves, as in 'stanch [*sic*] and sagacious activity.'

Of *flout* and *flaunt*, the former is the older, but only by a decade or so. Both are of uncertain parentage. *Flout*, 'to mock, defy, or show contempt,' is thought to be an extension of *floute*, a Middle English word that meant literally to 'play the flute.' Its Dutch cousin, *fluiten*, has gone through the same sense development.

Flaunt, 'to parade ostentatiously or flourish something flagrantly,' has a distinctly Gallic flair. But etymologists know of no French progenitor. The best guess is that it's a blend of *flout* and *vaunt*, with maybe a little *taunt* to boot. There's an element of audacity in both, so it's no wonder they've been confused from the beginning. Certainly it's possible to flout someone by flaunting something. There is a useful distinction between them, but it's usually easy to infer the intended meaning even when they're used 'incorrectly.'

So these perceived abuses are not as blatant as many people seem to think. Or should that be *flagrant*?

People have always said something like 'needless to say' before going right ahead and saying it anyway. It's a gimmick called paralipsis, and only the extremely literal-minded object to it.

SPEAKING OF THE INEFFABLE

S OME FRENCH PHILOSOPHER – I FORGET WHETHER IT WAS Descartes, Voltaire, or Marcel Marceau – once observed that when someone says 'needless to say,' you can bet your bottom sou that what follows is something that the speaker feels very much needs to be said. Judging by my mail, this apparent contradiction between phrase and purpose impels some literal-minded readers to the very precipice of apoplexy. 'If it's needless to say,' they write, 'why say it?' The question is, of course, rhetorical. And so is the phenomenon against which they fulminate.

It goes without saying (he said, proceeding nevertheless to say it) that there is a technical literary term for these eminently effable unmentionables. It is *paralipsis*, Greek for 'passing by omission.' There is also a variation known as *preterition* – known, that is, to people who get really deeply into this sort of thing, and speak a lot of Latin so that ordinary people cannot understand what they are saying, needless or otherwise.

Ordinary people just call it silly, not to mention ludicrous, to say nothing of absurd. But there is method in this apparent madness. With apologies to the nineteenth-century Scottish poet Alexander Smith, 'it is not of so much consequence what you do not say, as how you say it.'

To appreciate the rhetorical effectiveness of the device, try walking up to the gang at the water-cooler and saying, 'it goes without saying ...' or 'at the risk of beating a dead horse ...' Then clam up and walk casually away. Do you think they will continue their causerie as if you had not enigmatically interrupted? No, they will pursue you as a pack of starved schnauzers in whose midst you have dangled a tantalizing T-bone.

'*What* goes without saying?' they will bark, or '*Which* dead horse?'

It need hardly be added that, whatever the literal meaning of paralipsistic phrases, both utterer and utteree fully know there is more to come. Far from being superfluous appendages, the words that usually follow 'needless to say' really need to be said. In fact, they are accorded emphasis by the parenthetically cavalier treatment.

It is probably unnecessary to state that it is not a new trick. If the Greeks had a word for it, it is probably stating the obvious to assert that the Greeks used it. St Paul certainly did, as Tom McArthur points out in the *Oxford Companion to the English Language*. The apostle, in his epistle to the Hebrews (11:32), asks, 'And what shall I say more?' Then he goes on for another nine verses, or 185 words, which in paraphrase go something like this: 'Time does not permit me to mention Gideon, Barak, Samson, Jephthah, David, Samuel, etc.'

Paralipsis was formally defined as early as 1586, in a book called *The English Secretorie*, by Angel Day. We use it, he wrote, 'when in seeming to ouer-passe, omit, or let-slip a thing, we then chiefly speake thereof.' Chaucer used the device liberally. And it was not beneath Addison, Butler, Thackeray, Reade, and Dickens, let alone (another one!) that stalwart of plain spade-calling, George Orwell.

Nor is it only an English idiom-syncrasy. French has, among other expressions, *cela va sans dire*, which we borrowed word-for-word to make 'it goes without saying.' Germans use *es versteht sich von selbst* (literally, 'it makes itself understood') or the shorter but still mouth-filling adverb *selbstverständlich*. Italians handle it with *va da sè che*. At this very moment, people all over the world are saying things that ostensibly do not require articulation.

The Scots have two terse equivalents. In Sir Walter Scott's *The Bride of Lammermoor*, there is this: 'I hate fords at a' times, let *abe* when there's thousands of armed men on the other side.' *Abe* is an early form of the infinitive 'to be,' and *let abe* translates to 'let alone' as in 'not to mention.' Samuel Crockett's novel *The Raiders*, an 1894 saga about smuggling, has this sentence: 'No doubt he had many a sin on his soul, *forby* murder.' *Forby* is an obsolete English preposition and adverb that meant 'beside' or 'besides,' but in Scots has the broader sense of 'not to mention.' Both *abe* and *forby* still occur in Scotland and northern England.

Preterition is subtly more devious than *paralipsis*, in that its users feign silence while actually mentioning things that should not be spoken of. It can be demonstrated by this hypothetical hustings rhetoric: 'I could list all the shady deals my opponent has been involved in. But it would take far too much time, and I don't want to get down into the gutter with him. So I won't even mention it.' Needless to say, he already did.

The point is that there is no point in trying to make literal sense of these expressions. And please do not bother to write and thank me for this advice. In fact, don't mention it.

————————————   •   •   •   ————————————

Lovers of the English language owe a great 'dept' to the *Oxford English Dictionary*, in spite of its occasional – and commendably rare – typographical lapses.

NIGGLES IN A HAYSTACK

THE SHORT BUT FASCINATING HISTORY OF THE *OXFORD ENGLISH Dictionary*, at the front of the first volume of the second edition, provides a modest affirmation of humanity's – and the *OED*'s – fallibility. It allows that, after 120 person-years of proofreading, and probably the most intensive electronic checking, double-checking, and cross-checking in publishing history, the text of *OED2* was still susceptible of a 'residual error-rate' of 1 in every 250,000 characters.

The 350 million characters on 21,500 pages comprising the complete twenty-volume set make a formidable haystack in which to find these minuscule misprints. But Bradley Crawford, a Toronto lawyer who specializes in banking law, pricked his finger on one recently while browsing in the entry for *indebted*. Mr Crawford politely informed *Oxford* of his discovery, thus:

Dear Sir: I believe there is a typo on page 838 of Volume VII ... where one of the meanings of 'indebted' is given as 'in dept'. I assure you, I take no pleasure in drawing this to your attention. It is at most a trivial blemish that all will understand and forgive. One thought, however, continues to trouble me: the scholarship and reputation of your work are so great, the probability of error so small; do you consider there is any risk that 'in dept' will now become acceptable usage, apparently being sanctioned by the most respected authority on our language?

Within a sesquifortnight (*nonce-word*, invented for this nonce) Mr Crawford received an equally courteous reply from 37a St. Giles', Oxford, over the signature of John Simpson, co-editor, *Oxford English Dictionary*. He also got a free etymological opinion. 'Thank you for pointing out the typographical error in the *OED*'s entry for *indebted*, which we shall endeavour to correct at the next opportunity,' wrote Mr Simpson, who also expressed surprise because *p* is quite removed from *d, e, b*, and *t* on the keyboard.

As to your second question, whether 'in dept' will now become an accepted usage, it must be touch-and-go! The *b* in *debt* is itself an unnecessary letter, and originally did not form part of the word at all. The oldest records show *det(t)e* and similar forms as the Middle English spelling. The *b* was artificially introduced on analogy with the Latin *debitum*. So there is certainly a precedent for the respelling. On balance, however, I feel that the occurrence ... is not likely to have more effect on the language than the 1,917 other occasions in the Dictionary on which the word is spelled correctly.

Considering the 250,000-to-1 odds over-all, *debt* with 1 error in 1,918 fared rather poorly. But this niggle and whatever other typos there may be are mighty small molehills beside the mountainous masterpiece that is the *OED2*. It is, to be sure, an unfinished masterpiece, and always will be. The second edition, after all, was mainly an electronic merger of the 'Murray' dictionary, completed in 1928, and the subsequent Supplements. The editors updated where the need cried out, and they did add five thousand new items. But a lot, as they say in the short history, remains to be done.

'There is much in the style ... the punctuation, the capitalization, the definitional terminology, and the spelling (within entries and even of some headwords) that calls for modernization,' they admit. 'Many current words are illustrated by a latest quotation from the first half of the nineteenth century ... Recent examples ought to be supplied for every sense that is still current.' That is especially true of words near the top of the alphabet, naturally the earliest worked on by James A.H. Murray and his associates in the 1880s. The freshest quotation for *attitude*, as a frame of mind, is from 1876. Staler yet is the supporting material for *bathe* in its basic sense; the most recent citation is from Jedidiah Morse's *American Universal Geography* of 1796.

Edward Wilson of Worcester College, Oxford, found another niggle in the haystack, which he described in the March 1993 *Notes and Queries*. He was researching a sixteenth-century use of the participial adjective *fucking*, which appeared in a scrawled graffito in the margin of a copy of Cicero's *De Officiis*, called the Brasenose Manuscript. The anonymous notator expressed enmity for the scribe, John Burton, abbot of Osney, Oxford, by scribbling 'O d fuckin Abbot,' the *d* presumably a short form of 'damned.' He conveniently added the date 1528 to his rude scrawl, thus authenticating a written use of the profane intensifier that antedates the *OED*'s earliest citation by forty years.

But that is not what needled Mr Wilson. He noted that the *OED2* unabashedly lists, defines, and supports *the* 'four-letter word' (first recognized by *Oxford* only in the 1972 Supplement). But, he adds, the second edition contains a 'verbatim reprint from the original (1897) volume III of *OED*' for the intensifier *damned,* with the anachronistic comment, 'Now usually printed "d——d." ' That the *OED2* perpetuated this prissy Victorian propriety, yet ignored the fact that *fuck* and its derivatives are still often euphemized by dashes in print, Mr Wilson describes as a 'reprehensible failure.'

If so, it will – along with other shortcomings or long-in-the-tooth text – be remedied when the new Supplements start hitting the streets – at which point the haystack-hunt can, and no doubt will, begin all over again.

P.S. Called the *Additions Series,* the Supplements began appearing six months later, although volumes 1 and 2 did not redress the inconsistencies that attracted Professor Wilson's reproach. Volume 2 did display a questionable modernity by including 'grody to the max,' a US slang expression meaning 'unspeakably awful,' but I somehow doubt that this would appease Professor Wilson either.

At one time, my favourite typo in the *OED2* was in a citation supporting one sense of the entry for *medium.* It was the title of a 1967 work by Marshall McLuhan, given as *The Medium Is the Massage.* I pointed this out in a 'Word Play' column the day before I was scheduled to have lunch with John Simpson, who was visiting Toronto. As I shrank to the size of a toothpick, the *OED* editor quite matter-of-factly informed me that it was no typo – that McLuhan did write something with this title, spoofing the expression made famous in an earlier book, 'the medium is the message.'

Purists who fret when they see 'media' used as a singular noun are more concerned about bad Latin than good English. The singular 'media' has a meaning and legitimacy of its own.

THE MEDIA IS THE MESSAGE

I HAVE FEW DATA TO SUPPORT ME, AND MY STAMINA ARE NOT UP TO long, tedious research, but I have a hunch that *media* – the main agendum on many a pedant's plate these days – is well on its way to becoming a standard singular noun, except perhaps among hidebound literati and intransigent intelligentsia on various university campi, in style books and other blessed receptacles of holy semantic writ. My hunch also tells me that there are more people who use *media* as a singular noun than there are people who write bristling letters to the editor insisting on its immutable plurality – which is to say, a lot.

The media itself/themselves has its/their needle stuck in the old monaural groove. Most media style books (What! an adjective too?) stoutly maintain that *media* is a plural noun, period. The *New York Times Manual of Style and Usage* admits the existence of an alternative, but dismisses it as a subversive plot. '*Media* – still a plural, despite persistent efforts to turn it into a singular.' It adds, with a smug ivory-tower certainty, 'The singular is, of course, *medium.*'

The British Broadcasting Corporation's style guide is also stuck in the mud. Its diktat on *media* says this: 'Plural. "The media sometimes display (not displays) a sensational approach to events." Remember also that data, criteria and phenomena are plurals. But the plural of referendum is referendums, not referenda!' The (Toronto) *Globe and Mail Style Book* not only upholds *media*'s plurality, but includes within its wide network 'books, periodical publications, radio, TV, advertising, mass mailing.' How they managed to overlook town criers, tom-tom beaters, and smoke-signallers I do not know.

In a recent *Globe and Mail* column, a magazine critic was taking pot-shots at a gun-supporting US publication called *Women's Self Defense*. Among his targets was a cover story headline that read: 'How the Media Encourages Violence, Yet Discourages Women from Owning Guns.' 'The magazine,' he tut-tutted, 'is full of similar grammatical mistakes.' I could not detect any other solecisms, so I assumed he was taking aim at the use of the singular verb with the noun *media*. What these dauntless defenders of the *status quondam* fail to detect is that a linguistically fascinating, and utterly inevitable, semantic change is occurring – has already occurred, really – beneath their very proboscises (or *proboscides* for the classically rigorous). The result of this evolution is that there is now both a plural *media* and a singular *media*, and they each mean something different.

The legitimate and widely recognized singular meaning was illustrated recently in the *Globe and Mail*, despite the style book's taboo. The paper's television critic began a story this way: 'It is a mean, cold morning down at CHCH-TV, where the media has been invited to risk its collective life on the icy highway from Toronto to Hamilton [to review a series premiere].' The sense is clear and logical here. This *media* does not include book publishers and junk-mail pushers, and no reader would take that meaning. It means simply 'the news media,' or what used to be called 'the press,' used as a collective singular as early as 1797 (see *OED*, 'press n.,' 14).

The press served the purpose well, as long as it involved only 'print' media. When radio and television joined the club, some new collective handle was felt to be needed. My personal recollection is that workers in the parvenu 'electronic media' were the main movers of this change, even though they saw nothing incongruous in speaking of radio and television 'journalists,' or waxing verbally excited about 'tonight's headline stories.' The public, in its wisdom, accepted the nettlesome *media* – first used in this sense, to anyone's knowledge, in a 1923 article in *Advertising & Selling* called 'Class Appeal in the Mass Media.' In the same magazine, the singular *medium* appeared, but so did the singular *media*. And ever since, the purists have been more concerned about bad Latin than good English.

The language has a way of sorting out awkward situations, such as the ones created by the rather tortured 'proper' examples in the first paragraph. *Data*, still in transition, is usually singular outside academic and scientific settings. *Stamina* (plural of stamen) has been singular since the early eighteenth century when, like *media*, it developed a new sense. *Agenda* (which once had the singular *agend* in English) has been treated as one since the turn of this century. *Literati* and *intelligentsia* retain their snooty classical endings because it looks good on them and other pseudo-*cognoscente*. *Campi*, of course, is a joke.

Bacteria has just about completed its evolution to singularity. *Criteria* and *phenomena*, heard everywhere as singles, are encountering stern opposition from people who take care to speak of *a graffito*, but never say *a confetto*. Many of them also talk of *octopi*, unaware that the 'correct' Greek plural is *octopodes*, or that the accepted anglicized one is *octopuses* – the simple English plural *-s* or *-es*, as in *thesauruses, campuses, formulas, indexes,* and *memorandums*.

Mediums would have made sense, but early usage dictated the plural *media*. And, certainly, it is still a plural in such senses as 'various media are on display at the art show.' But *media* unmistakably has also taken on a monolithic unitary sense. I am happy to let the usually conservative *American Heritage Dictionary* have the last word: 'As with the analogous words *data* and *agenda*, the originally plural form has begun to acquire a sense that departs from that of the singular [*medium*]; used as a collective term, *media* denotes an industry or community.'

And that is pretty well the scoop on this issue.

——————————— • • • ———————————

POLITICS AND OTHER SHADES OF PRACTICE

The Speaker of the Alberta Legislature was absolutely right to prohibit the utterance of certain nasty words in that august chamber – although 'cowbell' might seem innocuous enough to the casual observer.

SPEAK PLAINLY WHEN YOU SPEAK ILL

S O 'CRAP,' 'BLATHERSKITE,' AND 'BOVINE EXCREMENT' ARE ON DAVID Carter's hit list. Good thing, I say. Bravo! And hear, hear!

Mr Carter, in case you missed it, is Speaker of the Alberta Legislature, and he was in the news because of his list of 172 words that he will not allow to be uttered in that august chamber. Mr Carter is obviously a champion of plain English, and he deserves the support of all who believe in clear communication.

It's a well-known fact that we are in the midst of a communications revolution, at least hardware- and software-wise. Faxes, cellular phones, satellites, semaphore, modems, smoke-signals, fibre optics, Morse code, videophones – who knows what lurks around the technological corner to aid us in our ever-intensifying itch to interface. Before long, by one estimate (mine), we will be spending twenty-three hours and fifty-five minutes of every day communicating or being communicated at.

So it's becoming more and more important that we fine-tune, reconfigure, streamline, reprogram, and down-size our vocabulary-ware – that is, the words we use to shape our ideas, our desires, our philosophies, and our pizza orders.

Miscommunication breeds misunderstanding, and this can be costly. Suppose you're barrelling down the highway and you hear a radio news report about an amazing new invention that will enable cars to run on ordinary tap water. You happen to hold a few thousand shares of Shell Oil, so you cellularly phone your broker and tell her to ditch the Shell stock. She says the bottom's fallen out of the petroleum market, and you might as well hang on to your Shell share certificates because they make nice bathroom wallpaper. 'Bovine excrement!' you shout into the phone, then violently jab the disconnect button. But she mishears you. She thinks you said, 'So buy Exxon.'

Well, you can easily see that this unfortunate and probably ruinous mix-up could have been avoided. If you'd just used the good old-fashioned, plain-English expression instead of that ludicrous euphemism for it, your broker would have got the message. And you would still be able to afford a cellular phone, along with a mobile cellular phone booth, which we used to call an automobile.

Same with *blatherskite*. This word deserves to be on Mr Carter's taboo list, if not for impropriety, then certainly for imprecision. If you want to call someone a bag of bodily waste, why on earth would you use such a quaint word, composed of archaic word elements like *blather* (bladder, or bag) and *skite* (Exxon)?

I wasn't entirely sure why Mr Carter saw fit to censor *crap*, until I sniffed around a bit in the *Oxford English Dictionary*. Now I realize that if you yell 'crap' in the Alberta legislative chamber, some Hon. Mems. might think you were referring to: a) husks of grain, or chaff; b) buckwheat; c) a weed that grows amid corn; d) residue formed in rendering, boiling, or melting fat; e) dregs of beer or ale; or f) thieves' slang for money. Obviously *crap* is far too open to misinterpretation to be used when you want to make your meaning perfectly clear.

So it seems that Mr Carter had ample reason to slam the lid on *crap*, and that his distaste for the word had nothing to do with the fact that Liberal leader Nick Taylor referred to him two years ago as 'the crappiest Speaker.'

I go along with Mr Carter on most of his rulings, but I can't blame the Alberta New Democrats for being miffed at his prohibition of the word *scab*. How would Mr Carter, an Anglican priest, like it if someone told him he couldn't use the word *sin*?

Some of Mr Carter's own staff expressed puzzlement at his proscription of *cowbell*. But in 1989 Mr Taylor – a mischief-maker, by all appearances – called a heckler a 'cowbell ... [with] the longest tongue and the emptiest head.' Now, some might consider this a folk metaphor of the highest order. And I have to admit it has an attractive ring to it. But metaphors should be confined to poetry, fine literature, oratory, and other respectable linguistic environments. As the plain-speaking Alberta Speaker has rightly ruled, they have no place in our legislatures.

———————————————   •   •   •   ———————————————

We're all familiar with bureaucracy, but how did this hybrid term – a mixture of French and Greek meaning 'rule by desks or offices' – become such a pejorative part of our vocabulary?

A HISTORY OF DESKTOP DESPOTISM

GOVERNMENTS COME AND GO, BUT THE BUREAUCRACY IS ALWAYS with us, steadfastly inaccessible, zealously devoted to the status quo, and resolutely dedicated to the proposition that all documents should be created equally obscure.

It must be said right off, to avoid offending one segment – albeit a very large one – of our society, that not all government workers are bureaucrats, and not all bureaucrats are government workers. You can find them at every level in banks, oil companies, universities, department stores, and even in powerful lobby groups whose avowed purpose is to stamp out the bureaucracy.

As James Boren pointed out in his delightfully depressing book *When in Doubt, Mumble: A Bureaucrat's Handbook* (1972), the state of the bureaucratic art 'can no longer be considered only the art of the state.'

We are not concerned here with the phenomenon, but with the word. How did this odd-looking foreign hybrid – a mixture of French and Greek meaning 'rule by desks or offices' – become such a commonplace, pejorative part of our vocabulary? Not surprisingly, it's a convoluted history.

Let's look at the *-cracy* part first. It's been traced to an Indo-European root *kar*, or 'hard,' which is also suspected of being the ancestor of the words *crab*, *cancer*, and *canker*. Who would have guessed that bureaucrats and crabs dropped from the same family tree?

In Greek *kar* became *kratos*, 'strength' or 'power,' and the Greeks formed a suffix *-kratia* to make such words as *aristocracy*, 'rule of the best-born'; *democracy*, 'power of the people'; *plutocracy*, 'government by the wealthy'; and *theocracy*, 'rule of god.' All the prefixes in those words had a combining form ending with a natural *o*, but later generations of word-coiners mistakenly read the suffix as *-ocracy* rather than *-cracy*. That led to such malformations as *mobocracy*, to which the mob answered with *snobocracy*; John Stuart Mill's *pedantocracy*; *landocracy*, and *clubocracy*; and in the twentieth century, *technocracy*, *meritocracy*, and the feminist creation, *phallocracy*.

The evolution of *bureau* is a case history in metonymy, a semantic process in which words develop meanings from associated things. In Old French there was a word *burel*, diminutive of *bure*, 'a coarse woollen cloth' (and in Modern French, 'a monk's habit'). A *burel* became specifically a cloth covering a desk, and as the spelling gave way to the modern *bureau*, it came to mean the desk itself. It broadened still further to denote the office in which the desk stood, and today – in English or French – can signify a whole collection of offices, and even the people who occupy them.

In the late eighteenth century, the French invented the word *bureaucratie* to describe the unelected apparatus of government. It was pejorative from the start, and it quickly made its way across the Channel to England. It was used in its French form as early as 1818, and by 1837 its spelling was fully anglicized when John Stuart Mill wrote of 'that vast network of administrative tyranny, that system of bureaucracy, which leaves no free agent in all France, except the man at Paris who pulls the wires.'

Long before, however, in the fourteenth century, that old coarse cloth, *burel*, had also migrated to England, where it became an adjective *borrel*, meaning 'unlearned' or 'of the laity.' This meaning degenerated to 'rough or rude,' and disappeared from general use in the nineteenth century, although it still exists in some dialects.

A rude or pushy bureaucrat is often described as *officious*, a once-complimentary word that has been turned upside-down, perhaps through association with uncivil servants. It's from the Latin *officiessus*, 'dutiful or obliging,' and had this meaning of kind attentiveness when it entered English in the mid-sixteenth century. Even as late as 1790, Edmund Burke wrote of people that they were 'well-bred, very officious, humane, and hospitable.'

But some people, too eager to please, went beyond the bounds of helpfulness, and into arrogant meddling, and the meaning of *officious* went with them. All of which proves, I think, that a few crab-apples can spoil the *burel*.

Was Bill Clinton's inauguration auspicious? There's an avian link in the origins of those two words, but that doesn't necessarily mean the new US president was given the bird of ill omen.

WORDS OF A FEATHER

I F A CONSPICUOUS INAUGURATION AUGURS WELL FOR SUCCESSFUL US administrations, that unstintin' Clinton commencement exercise was spectacularly auspicious. The four-day kick-off bash ended with the Rompin' Ronnie Hawkins Marine Band rendition of the traditional presidential salute 'Hi Y'all to the Chief.' And it gave me an excuse to write this inauguratory paragraph, which includes several words with some odd and ominous histories and relationships. Let's work backward and look first at *auspicious.*

Let's work so far backward that we find ourselves in sixteenth-century Europe – not a bad place to be, considering that you might run into the likes of Michelangelo, Catherine de Medici, Luther, Elizabeth I, Machiavelli, Spenser, Leonardo da Vinci, Lucrezia Borgia, or a gent named Shakespeare, whose influence on our language can scarcely be calculated. At the risk of being a party-pooper, I must say our potential celebrity list makes Bill Clinton's line-up look pretty blah (excepting, of course, the aforementioned Mr Hawkins).

The sixteenth century also saw the introduction into Europe of coffee, tobacco, and water-closets. So you can see that it was a very civilized and enlightened era indeed.

But for all its swingingness, the sixteenth century harboured some relics of the Middle Ages and earlier. Among these was a group of practitioners known as *auspices.* At the time, this was merely the plural of the word *auspex,* which came from the Latin *avis,* 'bird,' and *specere,* 'to observe.' So these occupational oddities were bird-watchers – but with a purpose.

There was usually an *auspex* in every village, sitting there pensively observing the flight formations and other activities of our feathered friends. People paid them good money for their advice, based on portents they divined from avian antics. Lest you be too quick to snicker, let me remind you that we still have teacup readers, economists, stockbrokers, palmists, pollsters, and political analysts.

These *auspices* did all right for themselves. Because they could read omens (there was a verb, *auspicate*, to describe this), they supposedly knew the most *auspicious* times and circumstances for important undertakings. Naturally, they were sought after as wedding consultants, and were often called upon to officiate at the actual splicings.

Those who could afford to get hitched under the auspices of an *auspex* were obviously hitching their wagons to a star. They were getting off to a propitious start, with influential patronage and authoritative sponsorship. And that pretty well sums up the meaning of *auspicious* or *good auspices* today.

Two synonyms for the now obsolete verb *auspicate* were *augur* and *inaugurate*.

Augur combined the same Latin *avis* with the first part of *garrire*, 'to talk,' from which we also got *garrulous*. (Some experts pin it on the Latin *augere*, 'to increase,' which spawned *augment*; but this theory doesn't fit today's tidy thesis, so ignore it.) In noun form, *augur* was an early job description for a Roman religious official who predicted the future from omens in the flight, feeding habits, and singing of birds, from the stars and planets, and sometimes from the entrails of sacrificial victims.

The verb has endured, and today a set of circumstances or a single occurrence may *augur* either well or ill. The word is often used loosely to mean 'signify.' Edward Bulwer-Lytton's *The Last of the Barons* describes a man 'whose open, handsome, hardy face augured a frank and fearless nature.'

Inaugurate was just a puffed-up version of *augur*, and puffed-up people still prefer it to the plainer *start* or *begin*. Originally it meant not only to read the omens, from whatever sources, but also to bless an enterprise or install someone ceremonially in an important office, often with a sacred purpose, just like the US presidency.

The adjective for all this falderal is *inaugural*, or at least it was until the early nineteenth century, when Americans started using it as a noun for the inaugural presidential address, or an opening speech at ribbon-cutting. Now it's a full-blown alternative for *inauguration* itself.

The ornithological occult has disappeared from modern inaugurals, replaced in most cases by platitudes, plebianism, and pleonasm. Often there are still things flying overhead, but the formations are now usually flocks of fighter aircraft. And come to think of it, there are probably some powerful portents there too.

_____   •   •   •   _____

A not-so-confidential memorandum to the prime minister–designate on the origins of some of the terms that cover governing. A 'cabinet,' for instance, was once just a little cabin – though not necessarily a log one.

CABINET-MAKING MADE EASY

MEMO TO: Prime Minister–Anoint
             Ottawa
SUBJECT: Cabinet-making

ONGRATULATIONS ON YOUR ELECTORAL VICTORY, MS PM-TO-be, and let's cut right to the chase. You were probably taking 'home economics' while the boys were at 'manual training' or 'shop' classes at Prince of Wales High. It occurred to me that if you didn't get to fool around with band-saws and lathes and drill presses when you were at school, you might *be* unaware of some of the finer points of carpentry or, more to the point, cabinet-making. Somebody right off is going to say that's a sexist remark. But that's the way things were in those days.

The first thing to remember is that there are different kinds of cabinets. It's probably obvious that a *cabinet* was originally just a small *cabin*. In the sixteenth century the word was used to describe a hut, a soldier's tent, a rustic cottage, or other small dwelling. It was even applied to the dens of beasts, as in this passage from *Peregrinatio Scholastica*, by John Day (1640): 'Where snakes and half-starved crocodiles made them sommer beds and winter cabinets.'

Naturally, that's not the kind of cabinet you want to be concerned with. Another difference is that the original one got smaller as time went by. From a little cabin or cottage, it became just a small room; then it shrank into a kind of case, or a piece of furniture, usually for keeping documents or valuables.

In its first political sense (around 1600) a cabinet was the private room in which the sovereign's advisers met, and before long it was used to describe the people rather than the room. Francis Bacon, among others, disliked the secrecy surrounding the practice, and called it 'a remedy worse than the disease.'

Cabinets, in the sense that we have tortuously arrived at, are made up of *ministers*, and there are different kinds of these too. *Minister* comes from the Latin *minus*, or 'less,' and in English it first signified a servant, agent, or underling, senses more or less preserved notionally in the modern church. But in the mid-seventeenth century, the word did a 180-degree turn when it was attached to a high officer of state, either a government department head or an envoy.

The most important minister is, of course, the *prime minister*, but your title-in-offing was not always one of respect. Perhaps because it was often used to describe the *sole* minister of a despot, the term was not generally accepted in Britain until the mid-nineteenth century. King Edward VII made it official in 1905.

You'll be handing out *portfolios*. About two hundred years ago English speakers called it a *porto folio*, from the Latin to 'carry leaves.' It was later changed to *portefolio*, giving it a more seemly Frenchness, but eventually it lost the *e*. Originally a case for carrying papers, drawings, maps, or music, *portfolio* has come to mean also a collection of stock shares or other securities. In 1800 or so, it was the term for a bag containing official government documents, and later for the office or responsibilities of a minister. A *minister without portfolio* can be in the cabinet, but can never be left holding the bag for a ministry.

You will have to give some thought to *committees*. It's interesting, but of debatable relevance, that a committee was originally not a group of people but an individual, as in *trustee*, *debauchee*, and *parolee*. In one early use, a committee was one to whom the care of a mentally incompetent person was assigned. The singular sense is archaic now, except in legal circles – but you, being a lawyer, would know that. Committees in the modern sense are useful for solving *ad hoc* problems, which they usually do by appointing a subcommittee or hiring a consultant.

I hope this helps to put a little historical perspective on the momentous task in which you are now engaged. Once you get over this first great hurdle, I would be only too happy to provide similar background to help you cope with such comparatively minor matters as national unity, debt, and unemployment.

————————————   •   •   •   ————————————

It's ironic that more than a third of the words in a fund-raising letter to fight bilingualism are of French origin. And it's sad that a City of Ottawa committee wants to ban 'racist' dictionaries.

WRITTEN IN BLACK AND WHITE AND FRENCH

TWO ITEMS OF AN INTRIGUING ETHNO-ETYMOLOGICAL NATURE:

1) Hand-delivered to my door in a plain white envelope was a fund-raising letter from the National Association of English Speaking Canadians. Neatly typed, grammatically passable, but enigmatically unsigned, the letter sought from me a cheque or money order to help the group 'promote and extend' its work.

I have a problem with this letter. I have read it carefully about ten times, and still I can't figure out what the group's 'work' is, or what is involved in promoting and extending it. Oh, it's clear enough the association has a gripe. 'For years,' the letter explained, 'the Federal Government of Canada has promoted the policy of [underlined] Official Bilingualism in an arrogant, heavy-handed and discriminatory fashion. The result is that many English Speaking Canadians feel that they are being treated like second-class citizens by their own government. This situation is clearly intolerable, and demands action.'

Alas, beyond the act of inscribing and mailing the aforementioned cheque or money order, there is no hint of what 'action' is required of me.

'Our method is simple,' the letter continues. 'One by one we are seeking out the support of English Speaking Canadians. People just like YOU. When enough English speaking people speak up, Ottawa will have to listen.' Alack, there is not a *soupçon* of a suggestion as to what we angry recruits, having drib-drabbed into a highly critical mass, are supposed to say, shout, scream, chant, or rap.

Although the word 'French' appears nowhere in the letter, the object of NAESC's discomfort is as plain as a pikestaff between the peepers. And as I read and reread this passionate plea, I was seized by a poignant sense of irony.

Of the letter's three hundred words, more than a third came into the English language from French. The proportion is even higher if you discount the repetition of Anglo-Saxon derivatives such as articles, prepositions, conjunctions, and forms of the verb *to be*. The imports include *government, politician, institution, official, language, arrogant, discriminatory*, and *second-class citizens*. Without French loan-words, the sentence, 'This situation is clearly intolerable, and demands action,' would read: 'This is, and.'

I idly wondered whether, at some point centuries ago, while most English speakers were busily and unbitchingly enriching their language with borrowings from French and other tongues, there was a National Association of English Speaking Englishmen. And did it send out begging letters aimed at financing a struggle against the linguistic Norman invasion?

My interest in the matter ended when I realized that, had such a lobby group not only existed but also been successful, the words *cheque* and *money order* would be Greek to me.

2) The City of Ottawa has a committee to advise authorities on matters concerning visible minorities. The committee made news recently by giving this advice: Get those racist dictionaries off our school and library shelves!

Committee members happened to be leafing through a few lexicons, with names like Oxford and Webster on their spines, when they discovered that the difference between *black* and *white* was like night and day. And they were not too vivified by *la différence*.

Under the entry for *black*, they found definitions suggesting, among other things, dirt, evil, sinister, and the colour of some people's skin. Under *white*, they discovered, among other things, definitions of innocence, fairness, cleanliness, and the colour of some other people's skin. Ipso facto: racism.

All I can say is, what took them so long? Maybe they've been too busy to ever look in a dictionary before, but you'd think *someone* would have brought this clearly intolerable situation (see Item 1) to their attention.

And race isn't the only 'ism' in these books. The dictionaries I have include broad, babe, doll, chick, filly, honey, and tomato, not to mention stud, stallion, wolf, Casanova, and Don Juan. There's codger, coot, geezer, fossil, and also hag, bag, bat, and battleaxe. Would you believe cripple, limp, lame, and halt? How about short, fat, ugly, and bald? From A to Z, they're litanies of scurrility.

So I'm with the committee. Let's give these handbooks of hate the old heave-ho – and lurn to liv in luv, peece, and blisfull ignerants.

———————————   •   •   •   ———————————

When the prospect of writing 'he or she or it' hundreds of times threatened to overwhelm efforts to modernize the statutes and regulations, Ontario's lawmakers did something daring.

EVERY MAN, WOMAN, AND CHILD FOR THEMSELF

T HE LAST PLACE YOU'D EXPECT TO FIND THE ROOTS OF QUIET revolution is in the august laws of the land. But only a few weeks ago, without a dissenting vote, the Ontario Legislature approved a bill that not only revised eighteen existing statutes, but also audaciously amended one of the precious precepts of English grammar.

In the blink of an 'aye,' Ontario's lawmakers legalized the wholesale use of the putatively plural pronouns *they*, *them*, and *their* to represent singular antecedents as in (*pace* Lord Nelson) 'Ontario expects *everyone* will do *their* duty.'

The wonder of it is that this bold and laudable reform happened more than three months ago, and there has been nary a howl of shock and appalment from the packs of self-appointed Cerberuses whose ears usually prick up at the slightest hint of deviation from some imagined code of correct language.

Although Ontario's elected politicians get the official credit for this enlightened move to rectify a long-standing deficiency in our language, the real moving spirit was Donald Revell. As Chief Legislative Counsel for Ontario, he is responsible for drafting the letters of the law, as well as the words they form.

The movement began in 1985, after the government sensibly decided to use gender-neutral language in all official publications. In 1988, Mr Revell and his staff began the daunting task of changing all existing acts and regulations to reflect the existence of two equal sexes among the governed.

They immediately collided with the pronoun problem. Ontario legal language followed the archaic convention of using the masculine pronouns *he*, *him*, *his*, and *himself* where the gender of the antecedent was uncertain, or could be either masculine or feminine. This hoary tradition reached its zenith of absurdity in 1984 when New York State politician Albert Bleumenthal said, 'Everyone will be able to decide for himself whether or not to have an abortion.'

In law, the pronoun problem is compounded by the fact that 'person' can mean individuals or corporations. So the current, cumbersome solution of replacing 'he' with barbarisms like 'he or she' or 'he/she' was made even more awkward by the addition of a third alternative, 'it.'

The Revell revisionists did resort to 'he or she' in many instances. They were sometimes able to solve the problem by simply repeating the nouns, or by recasting a sentence. These expedients are greatly favoured by style-book editors and other usage mavens who feel no amount of anguish is too great if it avoids offending venerated grammatical canons and their staunch, starchy supporters.

But the provincial law-writers encountered situations for which traditional English was simply inadequate. And they definitely drew the line at 'he, she, or it.' So they decided to let the third person plural pronouns do double duty as singulars, just as the second person 'you' has done for more than two centuries, after English users got tired of trying to keep the 'thou's' and 'ye's' straight.

An even thornier problem was the singular reflexive pronoun, which could be desexed only by replacing 'himself' with the truly tormented 'himself, herself, or itself.' The Revell drafters applied the same logic, and now the erstwhile solecism *themself* is part of the Queen's English (Ontario branch). It appears eighteen times in the revised statutes as a singular reflexive pronoun. Thus, for example, Ontario's Tobacco Tax Act says a consumer is 'any person' who buys tobacco 'for their own use' or for another principal who wants it for 'themself.'

Mr Revell doesn't see himself as an idiomatic iconoclast. 'It's not the job of legislation to reform language,' he says. 'At the same time, to resist change where a trend has become firmly established would not serve the principles of either sexual equality or plain language.'

The Revell reformers learned that the use of plural-cum-singular pronouns only became taboo on the whim of a handful of eighteenth-century grammarians, all men. They also found they were in pretty prestigious company, discovering examples in Chaucer, Shakespeare, the Bible, Byron,

Swift, Austen, and Orwell, to name a few respectable English users. Let your modern eye judge the following:

'And everyone to rest themselves betake.' – Shakespeare, *The Rape of Lucrece.*

'... if ye from your hearts forgive not every one his brother their trespasses.' – Matthew 18:35, *Authorized Version.*

'I would have everybody marry if they can do it properly.' – Jane Austen, *Mansfield Park.*

'Nobody here seems to look into an Author, ancient or modern, if they can avoid it.' – Lord Bryon.

'It is too hideous for anyone in their senses to buy.' – W.H. Auden.

'Every fool can do as they're bid.' – Jonathan Swift.

'Every person now recovered their liberty.' – Oliver Goldsmith.

'A person can't help their birth.' – W.M. Thackeray.

'We can only know an actual person by observing their behaviour in a variety of different situations.' – George Orwell.

'Each designs to get sole possession of the treasure, but they only succeed in killing one another.' – Sir Paul Harvey, *Oxford Companion to English Literature* (fourth edition, 1967).

'... unless a person takes a deal of exercise, they may soon eat more than does them good. – Herbert Spencer.

'I had to decide: Is this person being irrational or is he right? Of course, they were often right.' – Robert Burchfield, editor of the *Oxford English Dictionary* Supplements, and currently working on a revision of Fowler's *Modern English Usage.*

If you want more examples you can find them in Otto Jesperson's *Modern English Grammar* (1914).

——————————— • • • ———————————

ENGLISH AS A SUB-LANGUAGE

What did the advertising masterminds have in mind when they hit upon Chevrolet's brilliant new slogan? They say it means 'a commitment to a new way of life.' Oh?

A GENUINELY MEANINGLESS AD WORD

YOU MAY HAVE NOTICED THAT THE AUTOMONGERS AT GENERAL Motors have launched (to borrow a durable Madison Avenue verb) a massive media campaign with the catchline 'Genuine Chevrolet.' The advertising masterminds must have anticipated a few quizzically raised eyebrows, because in full-page ads this week the large-type catchline was immediately followed by the question, 'What is Genuine Chevrolet?'

And this was the answer: 'It's not a slogan. It's not just a theme. It's a commitment to a new way of life at Chevrolet.'

I don't know about you, but I found this response just a trifle unenlightening. In fact, it raised at least two more questions, which the Chevy people neglected either to ask or to answer: 1) Has somebody been hawking cheap, imitation Chevrolets at those street-corner stands, along with the ersatz Rolexes and mock Gucci bags? 2) If 'Genuine Chevrolet' means 'a commitment to a new way of life at Chevrolet,' has the company itself been flogging something other than the genuine article (not to be confused with 'the real thing,' which is another product – and another enigma – altogether)?

Both possibilities seem remote, so speculation is invited.

Is it possible the ad-writers consulted an unabridged dictionary and discovered that *genuine* originally meant 'natural, native, not foreign'? Is this a subtle, back-handed swipe at the imports? Not likely. This meaning of the word has been obsolete since the early eighteenth century, and few prospective car-buyers would make the domestic-import connection. Besides, not all Chevrolets are home-made, so this message, even assuming anyone got it, would be disingenuous.

The admen had plenty of alternatives, and they were all carefully considered. I know this, because 'Word Play' obtained a partial transcript of a meeting of the Ongoing Ad Hoc Strategic Thrust Task Group of the advertising firm of Blah, Blurb, Bafflegab, and Bletherskite (not its genuine name). Here it is.

Brad: Okay, basically we seem to be in agreement that *unvarnished*, *unadulterated*, *dyed-in-the-wool*, *honest-to-God*, and *the real McCoy* Chevrolet won't work. How about *Authentic* Chevrolet?

Chad: *Authentic*'s a good solid word, no question. But it makes me think of some old document, like a manuscript, or the Dead Sea Scrolls, or a Brian Mulroney doodle. Is that the image we want for the today's Chevrolet? We might just as well go for *indubitable* or *veritable* or *forsooth*. Hell, why not 'Chevrolet *Per Se*'? At least it rhymes.

Thad: Chad's got a point, Brad. We need a word that's very nineties. Not too flashy, not too slick. Respectable, but not ancient. Something decent, honest, sincere, sort of middle-of-the-infobahn. Something genuine.

Ahmad: Hey, that's real bad, Thad! Gen-yoo-wine! Got a nice ring to it. Kinda reminds you of *generous*, *gentle*, *genial*, *genius*, and *genesis*. Not to mention – heh, heh – *Gen*-eral Motors.

Vlad: And also not to mention *gen*-ocide and de-*gen*-erate.

Tad: We can always count on Vlad to go for the jugular.

Brad: Never mind him. I think I can sense a lot of support here for *genuine*. It's a fine word – a word that has stood the test of time. It worked for our spiritual forefathers, the much-maligned and misunderstood snake-oil salesmen. It worked for the beer company that successfully marketed 'genuine draft' beer in bottles ...

Chad: But isn't bottled draft beer a genuine oxymoron? Don't you think we've used *genuine* in so many artificial, contradictory, spurious, counterfeit, phoney, un-*bona fide* contexts that it's now utterly devoid of meaning? Like *unique*, *improved*, *recommended by*, and *much, much more*? Aren't we just going for *genuine* because it looks and sounds good, even though it means zilch?

Brad: You catch on fast, Chad.

———————————   •   •   •   ———————————

The actual smell of Father's Day fragrances seems to be quite beside the point. A browse in a beauty catalogue shows that psychology's the thing. And language is another thing.

IT'S THE ANALYSIS THAT COUNTS

PERSONAL AND CONFIDENTIAL MEMO TO JENNIFER AND JULIA: I know you're both very busy, and you probably haven't had time to even think about Father's Day, which is tomorrow. Fortunately, the people at the Eaton's store have thought a lot about it, and they were thoughtful enough to pass on some great ideas in a brochure called *Beauty Reflections.*

There was a woman in a bathing-suit on the cover, and a lot of stuff on feminine cosmetic products that help you get 'fabulous sun-kissed colour,' or make 'your own personalized summer shade statement,' or just 'sleek your skin' with a process called exfoliation, which I hope isn't as painful as it sounds.

But this flyer also had eleven pages aimed directly at men like me, through daughters like you. The section was headed 'Scents-ing It,' a personalized pun statement that I wish I'd thought of. The editors liked it so much, they gave it another clever twist in a subheading, 'Give dad a scents of fun.'

The advertisers themselves don't seem to know about the word *scent*, let alone *perfume, essence, bouquet, aroma, smell, odour,* or *stench.* The only odoriferous word they use is *fragrance*, or some novel form of it, as in 'fragranced soaps.' But I digress, as I'm sure you will be the first to point out, as usual.

Although the Eaton's folk have narrowed the field for you, I think you will still have to do some careful analysis of the various product plugs in order to choose the fitting fatherly fragrance for the pop in question.

You can probably eliminate some pretty quickly. XS Pour Homme (pronounced 'excess poor um'), for example, is a totally inappropriate 'sensual blend of fruity and floral notes, on a woody musk base,' which 'speaks of instinct and daring.' I'm not saying I don't like fruit, flowers, and woody musk, but surely fragrances should be sniffed and not heard – or at least not speak until spoken to. And I, for one, am not going to be asking many questions of my armpits or other fragranced bodily recesses.

You can also turn up your noses at Giorgio Armani's line, which 'offers a fresh blend of bergamot, enhanced by robust, spicy notes that evoke his complex personality.' As you know – certainly you mention it often enough – I have enough trouble suppressing various personality complexes, without having them evoked by some olfactive elixir.

Polo's got it all wrong too, in more ways than one. 'Whether he's chairing a meeting, he can wear Polo Crest or whether he's relaxing after a drink, he can wear Polo,' says Ralph Lauren's blurb. You know me well enough to realize I'd work myself into such a sweat just trying to parse that sentence that no fragrance could offset the damage.

Paloma Picasso has an attractive sounding one that allegedly is 'a unique ambery vanilla blend that captures the coolness of a sea breeze and the softness of a sunny garden.' Sounds nice, doesn't it? But why did she have to go and call it Minotaure, the French spelling for the Cretan monster with a man's body and a bull's head, who lived in a labyrinth and liked to eat little children. I just don't think that's me – although you might like to quibble over the bull-headed part.

We all know that advertisers usually avoid hyperbole, but I think Quorum is guilty of a slight overstatement when it says it 'combines leather and tobacco notes with green aromatics for a passionate, sensuous fragrance that every woman admires.' Leather and tobacco notes? It obviously hasn't consulted the three main females in my life (four if you count the cat).

I suppose if I belonged to a nudist colony, you could consider Azzaro Pour Homme which, according to its ad, 'is all he really needs to wear.'

I leave it to you to determine which combination of assertive, elegant, sophisticated, virile, bold, seductive, emotional, tender, spontaneous, refined, contemporary, and discerning describes me best. Heaven nose, there must be something that will add lustre to my lack. On second thought, maybe you could just phone.

Yours expectantly, Dad.

———————————   •   •   •   ———————————

Companions-wanted ads in newspapers raise all sorts of possibilities, not to mention eyebrows and questions, about whether one lovelorn lady really meant what she said.

IS SHE FRISKY, FESTAL, OR FLATULENT?

THE 'FRIENDS AND COMPANIONS' ADS IN THE WEEKEND GLOBE *and Mail*'s 'National Personals' section are – how shall I put it – somewhat tamer than some of the uninhibited mating calls that pass these days for lonely-hearts columns.

But my eyebrows, at least, were raised by a recent self-description by a Thornhill, Ontario, advertiser as an 'attractive, fiesty, sophisticated woman.' There was something familiar, but at the same time odd, about that word *fiesty*.

The closest thing in any of my dictionaries was *fiesta*, and I briefly entertained the notion that the lovelorn lady had coined an adjective meaning 'fiesta-like,' or convivial, jovial, gladsome, or festal. It occurred to me that the last word rhymes with *vestal*, and I considered for a rash moment that I had stumbled on a code word. Perhaps the *Globe* ads weren't as prudish as I had supposed. And maybe N/S doesn't stand for non-smoker?

It was about halfway through my second Saturday morning coffee that the penny of dull reality dropped with an unromantic clunk. It was just a misspelling of *feisty*, a word that is currently enjoying considerable vogue, and whose meaning has ameliorated considerably, not only over the past dozen centuries or so, but over the past three decades.

Journalists have fastened onto *feisty* as a vigorous and admiring adjective for, say, an elderly person who beats off a mugger, a smallish hockey player like Doug Gilmour who 'dishes it out' as well as takes it, or a pugnacious pol like Ross Perot or Sheila Copps. Synonyms for this new meaning include *spunky*, *frisky*, *spirited*, *gutsy*, and *courageous*. Sometimes there is a tinge of sarcasm, or euphemism, where *feisty* is either a disguised or polite way of calling someone bitchy. There is a thin line between mettlesome and nettlesome.

It must be assumed that the otherwise attractive and sophisticated Thornhill companion-seeker meant it only in the most self-complimentary way, unless she's as modest as the Calgary gent who described himself as 'almost handsome,' or the London SWM (single white male, I think) of 'average dimensions' who is looking for a 'somewhat intellectual soulmate.'

Thirty years ago, to call yourself or someone else *feisty* was downright disparagement. It meant disagreeable, touchy, overly aggressive, quarrelsome, or peevish – qualities more likely to attract SMs (sadomasochists) than SWMs.

But long ago, the adjective denoted a different kind of antisocial trait. In Old English, the onomatopoeic word *fist* had nothing to do with a clenched hand, but meant 'flatulence' or 'breaking wind.' It had malodorous relatives in the Germanic languages, which produced the modern German *fist* and the modern Dutch *vijst*, both meaning 'fart.'

The foul English *fist* lingered until the seventeenth century. In 1664, the Derbyshire poet Charles Cotton wrote in *Scarronides, or the Travesty of Virgil*: 'You might have heard his fist from one side of the skie to th' t'other.'

The word was applied figuratively to certain puff-balls, such as bullfist and wolves' fist, which had a habit of exploding when ripe. It also came to be used contemptuously to describe small, snappish dogs. In 1529, Thomas More's *Dialogue of Comforte against Tribulation* had a reference to 'a lyttle fysting curre.'

For some reason this canine connotation caught on in the United States, where the *fisting-hound* was well known in southern dialects. This derogatory term evolved into *fice*, *feist*, and even *foist*, and eventually produced the adjective *feisty*. The original windy meaning of the word was lost, but the new term, with its overtones of yappy irascibility, was being applied more and more to people. Around the turn of this century, *feisty* in the United States also acquired the sense of putting on airs, or flirting.

It's just possible there was a hint of this meaning in the ad placed by the would-be inamorata from Thornhill. It's also possible that she meant *fiesty*, in which case she's on her own.

But if she intended *feisty* in its fairly recent sense, she might want to open negotiations with the 'strong, gutsy, no-nonsense renaissance man' who also published his thumbnail autobiography in the *Globe*'s personal column. And she might ask him, for me, what *he* meant when he described himself as 'whitty.'

·   ·   ·

In the hustling decade of the 1990s, the ability to lounge around on a front porch may be a lost art. 'Porch' comes from Latin, naturally – the Romans were good at leisure.

NEEDED: EXPERIENCE IN CREATIVE INERTIA

'A COUNTRY HOUSE WITHOUT A PORCH IS LIKE A MAN WITHOUT an eyebrow,' wrote the American ruralist D.G. Mitchell in 1867. I'm not sure I fully grasp the analogy, but it's interesting to note that these agreeable architectural add-ons – the porches, that is – are making a comeback.

One Toronto building firm is advertising porches as the *pièces de résistance* of its new line of domiciles. This is a welcome development, but I wonder whether the current generation of hustling, harried home-buyers has enough experience in creative inertia to practise the art of dynamic do-nothingness.

We have a lot of strange words for those residential areas where, season permitting, it's nice to let get-up-and-go give way to sit-down-and-vegetate. *Porch* is the oldest and most prosaic of our terms for these places of pure, unagitated languor. In Old English it was *portic*, formed on the Latin *porticus*, which also sired *portico*. Today's spelling more closely follows the Norman French version *porche*, which arrived in the fourteenth century.

But *porch*, in this sense, is strictly North American. In Britain, a porch is a taller structure sheltering the approach to a building's entrance – something that would comfortably cover a coach-and-four or a passel of Porsches (no relation). In northern England, *porch* also describes the transept or side chapel of a church.

Even here in North America, agreement on its meaning is not unanimous. In Atlantic Canada and parts of New England, the porch is a utility or storage room at the back of the house, usually leading to the kitchen. I can't recall what a *porch* was in London, Ontario, a half-century ago, but we called the covered platform at the front of a house – a kind of theatre-in-reverse where the audience sits on the stage and watches the play unfold beyond – a *veranda*.

The old Spanish or Portuguese word *baranda*, a 'railing' or 'balcony,' first travelled to India, where it infiltrated Hindi and Bengali. From there, it made its way into English around 1700. *Veranda*, like *porch*, means different things on different English tongues. In Australia and New Zealand, it is understood to denote a roof-like structure, or permanent awning, covering the sidewalk in front of businesses.

While verandas and porches may be just poising for a comeback, their high-rise counterparts have long been enjoyed by apartment-dwellers. These airy aeries are named after the Italian *balcone*, a fancy version of *balco*, or 'scaffold.' The best-known *balcony* in English is the one under which Romeo wooed Juliet, even though the word was never used by Shakespeare. The earliest written record of *balcony* in English is dated 1618, two years after the Bard's death.

The Italians have generously allowed us to use two other words for sites of quiescent scenery-watching. *Belvedere*, a latticed wooden garden structure that also seems to be enjoying renewed popularity of late, is from *bel*, 'beautiful,' and *vedere*, 'view.' It's sometimes called a *pergola*, although this word more accurately describes a trellis or arbour for trained plants, which is its meaning in Italian.

Perhaps the most common current word for this garden grandstand is *gazebo*, which looks Italian, but isn't. The exotic contexts of its early mentions in English, in the mid-eighteenth century, suggest an oriental source. But most word experts believe it's just a fanciful invention based on the verb *gaze*, with a Latinate first person future ending, as in the genuinely Latin *videbo*, 'I shall see.'

Looking back toward the house, what we see is a *terrace*, a word with a long and interesting history. Its ancestry goes back to a prehistoric root *ters*, 'to dry.' Through various evolutionary skeins, this root grew into our modern *thirst*, *toast*, *torrid*, and *torrent*. (The last, despite its modern association with water, comes from the same root, Latin *torrere*, 'to scorch,' as *torrid*. The water connection developed when the 'burning' sense changed to 'boiling.') The ancient root *ters* produced the Latin *terra*, 'dry land,' or 'earth,' and *terrace* is one of its many derivatives. It actually came directly from a Latin adjective, *terraceous*, 'earthy.'

Having trudged up the *terrace*, we might pause on the *patio*, but not for long, because this is customarily the scene of rather more vigorous activity – barbecues, cocktail parties, lawnmower repairs – than that associated with the other members of today's collection. Whereas the English *patio* adjoins the house, usually at the rear, its Spanish forebear is an inner courtyard, completely enclosed by the house.

D.G. Mitchell may not have known it when he penned his paean to the porched country house, but domestic architecture already had a feature named for those bushy facial prominences. They were decorative mouldings over windows, known as eyebrows – a disclosure which may or may not raise any human ones.

———————————   •   •   •   ———————————

An engine was originally a product of ingenuity. Then it became a battering-ram or war machine, and later an industrial powerhouse. Now it's a robotic digester of digital data.

ENGINES: A CIRCULAR TRACK RECORD

A COMPUTER SOFTWARE COMPANY WITH THE FAIRLY PRETENTIOUS name of SAS Institute Inc. has a 'new concept' for creating and using electronic data files, which it calls 'Multiple Engine Architecture.' I couldn't bore you with the details if I wanted to, because I don't understand them. But I do gather from the institutional literature that the guts of this concept, or product, is something called the 'V608 Engine.'

Now, I know you're just dying to zoom out to your nearest showroom to kick some wires and ask the salesperson, 'What'll she do?' (zero-to-sixty MHz in four nanoseconds). But stay a moment, while we reflect that the word *engine*, for all its mechanical connotations, has a certain cerebral background that is not entirely inappropriate when applied to an electronic brain in this post-modem era.

We can trace *engine* back to the Indo-European root *gene*, 'to beget or give birth.' As it turned out, this was a potently prolific progenitor. To list all of its offspring would take up most of the rest of this space, so we'll look at just a few. Through the filter of Latin, we have *gender, general, generate, generic, generous, genius, congenial, degenerate, genuine, ingenuous, germ, germinate, German, genital, benign, pregnant, nation, naive, natal, nature, native*, and *renaissance*. From Latin via French came our *gentile, genteel*, and *gentle*. Through Germanic channels we received *kin, king, kind*, and *kindergarten*. And thanks to a Greek twist our language now has *genealogy, genocide, homogeneous*, and *gonad*.

Two other Latin offshoots that sprouted in fourteenth-century English were *ingeny*, a now obsolete word that meant 'mind, intellect, or disposition,' and the closely related *engine*, one of whose early meanings was 'native talent, inborn wit, or just plain genius.' If the *engine* was misused, it could also mean 'cunning, trickery, or skill in contriving.' Another old word for the latter was *malengin*, sometimes Freudianly rendered *male engine*.

The noun *engine* also represented the product of ingenuity, a 'contrivance or device.' It could also denote a 'plot, ruse, or snare,' eventually leading to the truncated modern *gin* for 'trap.'

An extension of the 'device' sense soon led to mechanical things such as tools and machines. Since some of the really impressive hardware then, as now, related to warfare, *engines* were commonly battering-rams, catapults, and other offensive ordnance. Even more horrific is King Lear's simile, 'like an engine, wrencht my frame of nature from the fixt place' – a comparison to a torture rack, another ingenious *engine* of the past.

By the mid-seventeenth century *engine* had generalized to include any more or less complicated contraption with several working parts, designed for a specific purpose. It could be a clock, a mill, or a knitting-machine. The Industrial Revolution, kick-started by the steam-engine, eventually produced the internal-combustion engine and, more recently, the SAS V608.

So *engine* has come tortuously full-circle, from native wit and genius to a redoubtable robotic digester of digital data. Its *curriculum vitae* exemplifies the marvellous resilience of English, and makes me wonder why so many people get their noses so far out of joint when a word takes on a new or expanded meaning.

Take *gender*, for example, just to keep it in the *gene* family. *Gender*, we are told authoritarianly, does not refer to the male or female sex, but to the masculine, feminine, and neuter properties of various parts of speech. It's a grammatical term, you numbskulls!

Well, it all depends on how stuck-in-the-mud you want to be. A real reactionary would insist on *gender*'s original English meaning. From the Latin *genus* and the Old French *gendre*, 'race or kind,' in fourteenth-century England it was a synonym for 'kind, sort, or class.' Later, when Hamlet referred to the 'general gender,' he meant the common folk.

There are records of *gender* references to male and female humans in the fourteenth century, but the grammatical sense didn't gain currency until the early 1500s. So its recent use, generated by feminists but now in general circulation, is neither new nor illogical. It doesn't take much native wit, or a high-powered electronic engine, to figure that out.

———————————————   •   •   •   ———————————————

Language finesse may be lacking among the sportscasters, but unconscious wit and perhaps even comatose waggery abound – that is, if you have a high tolerance for the 'noise-level factor.'

THE GLOBAL WORLD OF 'SPORTS TALKERS'

M Y JAUNDICED EYE WAS ARRESTED BY THE HEADLINE IN A sports-page ad from the National Institute of Broadcasting. 'Sports Talkers Wanted,' it said, and in smaller type added, 'no experience needed.'

It occurred to me that this ad might be a manifestation of a new advertising policy combining honesty and plain language. True, there was still something a little ambiguous about the 'no experience needed' line. Did they mean no experience in 'sports talking' or no experience in anything – including English? Surely, I thought, that's carrying candour too far.

Still, to anyone who listens to 'sports talkers' on television, it's hard to escape the conclusion that knowledge of English words, grammar, and idiom is not only not 'needed' but actually frowned upon. On the other hand, unconscious wit and comatose waggery, of which there is nary a mention in the National Institute of Broadcasting ad, abound in the broadcast booth.

In a Canadian Football League game last fall, sports talker Joe Galat said, 'it's tough sledding there in the trenches.' The casual 'sports listener' might have dismissed that as a routine mixed metaphor, overlooking the subtle fact that one of the teams was the Edmonton Eskimos.

My favourite grid guru is Dan Kepley. In one match he noted that Ottawa pass receivers were 'not running any type of intermediary rout,' possibly because their opponents displayed a 'very linebacker-oriented-type' defence. He added that the whole Ottawa attack was based on 'the same old plays with some improvisions [*sic*] in them.' Who would have thought Mr

Kepley capable of resurrecting a long-obsolete word meaning 'lack of fore-thought'?

In the same game, the jock-ular Mr Kepley informed us that the Win-nipeg coach was calling the plays for quarterback Matt Dunnigan 'so he [Dunnigan] doesn't have to put a lot of thought process into it.' Tennis players, however, are always on their own, thinking-wise. And sometimes, as TSN talker Peter Burwash noted, 'Your entire thought process – both physically and mentally – is off.'

The 'noise-level factor' can be particularly unnerving at the beginning of a game when, according to an American talker, 'all that anxiety is taking place.' And the first game of a play-off series can be a real nightmare. Toronto Maple Leafs coach Pat Burns says that's when 'all the nooks and crannies are out.'

Sports talker Wes Hicks spotted a player who had obviously figured out a way to avoid tough trench-sledding. The player, he said, 'never stops his legs moving; they're always constantly going all the time.' Sort of like sports talkers' mouths.

Some observations are blindingly insightful, like this one about a team hopelessly behind with only minutes remaining in the game: 'It's going to be hard for them to maintain their winning streak after this loss.' Or this titbit, from the CBC's Rick Cluff, about the Tour de France: 'Runner-up Tony Romminger placed second.'

Others are so profoundly droll that they take moments to sink in. Like the one in which a talker noted that at the Orange Bowl in Miami, 'the field is very close to the stands – and vice versa.' Or the observation that the British Columbia Lions 'have absolutely nothing to hold their heads low about.' Or the Wimbledon tennis match where the camera focused on a woman spectator wearing a Chicago (basketball) Bulls cap, and talker Barry McKay intoned, 'We live in a global world, don't we?'

A few weeks before that, we saw pictures of people in a long queue at Roland Garros Stadium in Paris. Sports talker Dick Enberg said some of them had been there since the day before, and that their patience had been rewarded by 'a standing-room-only seat at the final of the French Open.'

Many sports talkers are former professional athletes, and I have a strong suspicion that superjock Eric Lindros is already in training for a post-hockey sports-talking career. After Canada's close victory over Czechoslovakia last year, he declared: 'I don't think the score was vindicative of the game.'

Well, as TSN talker Paul Romanuk said after updating us on a baseball game being played elsewhere, 'We'll continue to keep our eyes peeled closely on that one.'

_____   •   •   •   _____

If it's whammo adjectives you want – and exclamation points!!! – turn to the real estate ads. You'll open the door on a world that's fantastic, fabulous, divine – and, when you get right down to it, lofty!!!

THE UNREAL WORLD OF REAL ESTATE

IF YOU'RE LOOKING FOR SHEER, INCREDIBLE, BOLDLY CONTEMPORARY, incomparably unique, totally unsurpassed excitement in your newspaper, nothing – and I mean nothing!!! – beats the real estate pages.

I don't know about you, but exclamation points really get my adrenalin coursing. My blood, too! The more, the hairier. They make my nares flare, and cause incipient varicose veins to balloon like a libidinous bullfrog's throat.

And no advertisers out-exclaim the realtors. In this febrile field, they're rare, one-of-a-kind, exceptional, outstanding, superb, fantastic, fabulous, spectacular – and stunning!!! The punctuational ejaculations don't just come singly, either, like in those wimpy movie ads, or Mel Lastman's (Mayor of North York) press releases. In the unreal world of estate-mongering, a single exclamation point is as flat as a full-stop. The valiant but solo exclamation mark can do little to energize 'S. of Lawrence, W. of Yonge!' And it's not difficult to stay fairly calm in the face of '30 Wellington St. East!'

But the double whammo-ed 'New Listing – Alamosa Area!!' sets off little tremors of excitement, and 'Lawrence Park – Reduced for Quick Sale!!!' raises the exclamatory oomph to the power of three and quickens the pulse measurably. If I ever hit upon a four-banger – or vice versa – I'm sure the old sphygmomanometer will spin right off the scale.

And how about those adjectives! Simply Superlative!! The Ultimate!!! And don't just take my word for it. The apotheosistic modifiers, like the mint-condition or lovingly restored domiciles they describe, are a must-see! Many are magnificent and some are rare, exquisite, gorgeous, and immaculate. A few are handsome, darling, or cute, but many more are luxurious, prestigious, and sumptuous, or have panoramic, dramatic, charming, or picturesque views. On these pages the classic and stately rub shoulders with the trendy and exciting. Some are spacious, yet gracious, proving that real estate copywriters can rhyme, if not reason.

A lot of pretty pedestrian properties are merely perfect. To stand out from the crowd, a home (never, never a *house*!!) must be 'absolutely perfect,' with at least two exclamation points. Unless it's divine.

Seasoned scanners can instantly recognize the nudge-nudge, wink-wink behind such phrases as 'loads of potential!' and 'ready for your personal touch!' And the adperson who penned the modifier 'extra ordinary' is a genius of audaciously ambivalent subtlety. But I can only assume that the agent who tried to pump up a million-dollar Forest Hill *pied-à-terre* with *pretty, great,* and *nice* was just having an 'extra ordinary' day.

I think I could use some interpretive help with 'cathedralized ceilings' and 'ravine-like lot.' And there is almost certainly a hidden message in the ad for the 'perfect little pad' within walking distance of 'financial core and hospitals.' I believe I'd feel more comfortable going 'very, very uptown,' even though I have no idea what it means.

Some of these domiciliary descriptives exude Victorian Elegance and Old World Charm. Some evoke an even earlier age (say, Stone?), such as the Gardener's Delight that also offered a 'garage for the craftsman, custom kitchen for the lady.'

Judging by the frequency of mention, the most sought-after qualities are roominess, privacy, uniqueness, comparability to a gem – and above all, quiet!!! That being the case, I question the wisdom of admitting that an 'incredibly renovated' house in Toronto's opulent Forest Hill area has 'all the Bells and Whistles.' Children's safety is, of course, a prime concern of many, but I personally wouldn't find much security in a street described as a 'child safe dead end,' and I'm not sure that a 'fantastic child safe street' fills me with confidence either.

Having had a couple of less than splendid experiences with backed-up drains in my present location, I'd also be a bit wary of something touted as 'floating in light and space.'

Note to real estate persons: I am not looking for a new house, or home, or residence. Honest! Not even if it *is* 'Kingsway cute' or 'Cricket Club gorgeous.' Don't call me; I'll call you. Just be assured that when and if I *am* in the market, I'll be looking for something that is – as one of you so exquisitely put it – 'more than a lifestyle statement!!!'

I can't leave the Disney world of real estate advertising without mentioning two of the most historically fascinating words in that lyrical lexicon – penthouse and loft.

Penthouse has certainly come up in the world, and a dizzying and tortuous climb it has been. It's rooted in the Latin *appendere*, 'to hang or add something onto something else,' from which we got our modern words *pending*, *append*, and *pendulum*. The modern French *appendre* has the same meaning as the original Latin. A medieval past participle, *apentiz*, signified a low shed or lean-to with a single sloping roof, set against another building. It too survives in modern French as *appentis*, with the same humble meaning.

Many English words reached their present form through a process called aphesis (from Greek *aphienai*, 'to let go'), in which a short, unstressed first syllable is dropped in speaking, then gradually disappears in writing. *Cute* got cut from 'acute,' and *squire* from 'esquire.' *Raiment* was tailored from 'arrayment' and a *longshoreman* is a lopped version of an 'along-shore-man.' In the same way, the lowly French lean-to, *apentiz*, became in English *pentiz* or *pentis*.

With no etymologists or 'Word Play' columns to set them straight, people naturally but mistakenly began to associate the slope-roofed outhouse with a different French word, *pente* or 'slope,' and by the sixteenth century, folk etymology had transformed the second syllable *-is* into *house*. In Samuel Johnson's 1755 dictionary, *penthouse* is defined as 'a shed hanging out aslope from the main wall,' and as late as 1840 in *Barnaby Rudge*, Charles Dickens described Fleet Market as 'a long irregular row of wooden sheds and penthouses.'

Over the years, *penthouse* has covered a number of subsidiary structures, such as porches, covered walkways, the eaves of a roof, or a small roof-ledge projecting over a door or window to provide shelter from rain. It was not until this century, and the advent of high-rise buildings, that the word began to ascend the social scale.

The third edition of the *American Heritage Dictionary of the English Language*, an improvement over an already excellent product, contains more than four hundred history notes on etymologically interesting words. One of these explains the upwardly mobile modern meaning of *penthouse* this way: 'The use of the term ... developed from the application of the word to a structure built on the roof to cover such things as a stairway or an elevator shaft. *Penthouse* then came to mean an apartment built on a rooftop and finally the top floor of an apartment building.'

A trendy near-synonym for penthouse is *loft*, a word that started out on a much higher plane, but eventually came down to earth – or almost so.

In Old English it was *lyft*, ancestor of our modern *lift*, and it meant the 'sky,' the 'air,' or the 'heavens.' Modern German *Luft* (as in Lufthansa) and Dutch *lucht* also mean 'air.' In late Old English, the word became *loft*, influenced by the Old Norse word of the same spelling, denoting 'air,' 'sky,' and – significantly – 'upper room.'

But the sense of an upper chamber or attic didn't appear in English until the fourteenth century, when it began to be used to denote a compartment over a stable, usually for storing hay. In time it expanded to include a gallery in a church, where the organ was located, and sometimes the choir. At one point, it signified any storey of a building other than the ground floor, and this sense developed in the United States to mean a large, unpartitioned, upper floor of a factory or warehouse.

Sometime around the mid-1960s, many lofts in Manhattan began to be converted into airy artists' studios. This gave a chic cachet to the erstwhile utilitarian quarters, and before long they were in demand as fashionable digs, almost on a par with penthouses, but – ironically – not quite as lofty.

These two words for a prestigious pad – one that clambered up from a back alley and one that descended from the clouds – now share a posh and pricey position in realtors' rhetoric.

• • •

GHOSTS, HOLY AND OTHERWISE

Here is fodder for seasonal small talk as you steer an unsuspecting buss-ee toward that sprig of ancient Christmas custom we call mistletoe. (In keeping with the mood, you might want to omit the 'turdus' part.)

WHY WE DON'T KISS
UNDER THE HOLLY

I SEE THE GREENGROCERS ARE STILL STOCKING MISTLETOE — AT $1.99 a sprig this year, or 79 cents for a fetching silk and plastic version — so I assume our current obsession with hygiene has not yet put the kiss of death on one of the oldest of Christmas customs. In fact, myths and rituals associated with the parasitic plant predate Christianity, and not all of them were as frolicsome as the osculatory observance familiar today. The word *mistletoe* itself is an oddity. What is a *mistle*, and what's so special about its *toe*?

In Old English, mistletoe was just *mistel*, a word borrowed from Old High German *mistil*, named after a bird we now call the missel thrush. This bird, which has a liking for the viscous mistletoe berries, and propagates the plant by depositing seed-laden droppings on various trees, probably got its name from an Indo-European root *meigh*, meaning 'to urinate.' Its Latin name, *Turdus viscivorus*, perpetuates the connection with biological waste. And so does the related modern German word *Mist*, or 'dung.'

But it is bootless to look for any pedal association in the *toe* part. In Anglo-Saxon times, the plant was also commonly known by the longer word *misteltan*. *Tan*, meaning 'twig,' evolved into *toe*, perhaps through the charm-ing corruption of folk etymology. It could just as easily, and perhaps more logically, have ended up *misteldew*, its sometime name in the seventeenth century. This would at least have had the virtue of consistency with its ancient liquid ancestry.

Few other growing things have been the object of more reverent and dreadful superstition. In 1600, playwright Robert Greene wrote that mistle-toe was so toxic that 'none comes neere the fume [of it] but he waxeth blinde.'

A dozen years earlier, Shakespeare's *Titus Andronicus* had a line describing trees as 'o'ercome with moss and baleful mistletoe.'

This poisonous reputation came from one of the great tragedies of Norse mythology. Balder, son of Odin and Frigg, was the fairest and wisest son-of-a-god around. After he had some premonitory nightmares, his mother, the aforementioned Frigg, made everyone and everything on earth swear an oath not to hurt him – everything, that is, but the mistletoe, which she considered too inconsequential to do anyone harm. Loki, the god of mischief, tricked Balder's blind brother, Hod, into flinging a sprig of 'baleful' mistletoe at the not-quite-invulnerable Balder. That proved to be his Achilles' heel, if I may mix mythologies, and invite charges of Balder-dash.

But mistletoe has also had its admirers. It was the 'Golden Bough' of Virgil's *Aeneid*, and it was much valued as a medicine for many centuries. In 1663, the physicist-theologian Robert Boyle wrote of 'a young lady [who] was cured onely by the powder of true misseltoe of the oake.' In 1723, a physician named Sir John Colbatch wrote a whole book on the subject, called *A Dissertation Concerning Mistletoe; A Most Wonderful Specifick Remedy for the Cure of Convulsive Distempers*. Here's a sample from it: 'It very commonly happens that Epilepsies, and other Convulsive Disorders, are not original Diseases, but Symptoms and Consequences of some other Distemper or Accident. As for instance, Worms corroding the most sensible Membranes of the Guts, impassible Stones in the Ureters, wounded Nerves and Tendons &c. Mistletoe will frequently relieve People under all these Circumstances ...'

Colbatch thought mistletoe little less than miraculous, and gave recipes for potions that even poor people could afford. Following is a 'cure' for asthma: 'Four Ounces of bruis'd Mistletoe to be infus'd in a Quart of boyling Water for an Hour, then to be strain'd out, when perfectly cold to add half a Pint of *Lisbon* White-wine; afterwards, with two Ounces of blancht Almonds to make an Emulsion, and to be sweeten'd with a sufficient Quantity of fine Sugar.' Cheers!

In another book, the 1866 *Treasury of Botany*, John Lindley and Thomas Moore wrote that 'mistletoe of the oak had such repute for helping in the diseases incidental to infirmity and old age that it was called *Lignum Sanctae Crucis*, Wood of the Holy Cross.' All over Europe, right down to the nineteenth century and no doubt in many places still, people believed mistletoe cured everything from epilepsy to hoof and mouth disease, and rendered barren women and cattle fecund.

The curative symbiosis of mistletoe and oak derives from the Druids, who believed the mystic growth was planted on the sacred oak by the god of lightning. In the most solemn Druidic ritual, a left-handed priest, wearing a white robe and wielding a golden sickle, cut the mistletoe. It was carefully caught in a white sheet, because it must not be allowed to touch the ground. Then a fatted ox or, if the gods really needed appeasing, an ill-fated human was sacrificed.

Kissing under the mistletoe is also a pre-Christian custom. Because it was not rooted in earth, the plant symbolized freedom from inhibitions. During the pagan yuletide, various liberties were permitted people who happened to be, or contrived to be, situated under a sprig hung from the ceiling or door lintel. After each hanky or panky a berry was plucked, and when they were all gone, that was the buss terminal.

This procedural rule is no longer observed, but it's nice to see that some of mistletoe's magic survives.

———————————   •   •   •   ———————————

When you discover that words such as 'placebo' and 'patter' have ecclesiastical roots, you may think you know why, but you might just canter to the wrong conclusion.

YOU SAY MUMPSIMUS, I SAY FORGET IT

FOR REASONS THAT ONLY THE MOST DILIGENT OF FELLOW-ditherers could appreciate, I found myself recently deep in the 'M' department of my electronic Oxford, trying to discover whether it is possible linguistically, if not medically, to have only one measle or one mump.

Evidence that singular versions of these ailments did indeed at one time exist – although it's hard to imagine anyone being seriously inconvenienced by 'a measle' or 'the mump' – gave only momentary gratification. What riveted my attention, and provided a focus for a further three hours of dilatory delving, was the entry just down the page from *mumps*.

It was *mumpsimus*, and it is defined as 'one who obstinately adheres to old ways, in spite of the clearest evidence that they are wrong; an ignorant and bigoted opponent of reform; an old fogey.' It can also be a tradition or notion stubbornly adhered to, or an adjective for 'stupidly conservative.'

What a wonderful word! And even more delightful is the tale behind it. The story is told, along with many other charming anecdotes and fascinating vignettes of British history, in a book called *Remains Concerning Britain*, by the historian William Camden.*

The story, dated AD 1517, was first recounted by Richard Pace, secretary to Henry VIII. An illiterate old English priest was overheard muttering *quod in ore mumpsimus* in the Eucharist instead of *quod in ore sumpsimus* (what

---

* An excellent edition of this wonderful book was published by the University of Toronto Press in 1984. R.D. Dunn, of Vancouver, who has taught English literature at the University of Toronto, Université Laval, and the University of British Columbia, edited this edition.

we have taken into our mouths). When the error was pointed out to him, he haughtily replied, 'I will not change my old mumpsimus for your new sumpsimus.' Thus the headstrong holy man went down in the annals of fogeydom.

The expression must have enjoyed almost overnight popularity. The great Bible translator and reformer William Tyndale, in his scathing attack on the church called *The Practyse of Prelates*, in 1530, used it to denigrate members of the bar: 'The chauncelars of England ... which be all lawers and other doctoures mumsimusses of divinytie were called upp sodenlye to dispute the mater.'

Mumpsimus, of course, is not on the tip of everyone's tongue. But a number of other words have sprouted in our everyday vocabulary from religious roots. For example, the verb *patter*, 'to speak rapidly or glibly,' as in a sales pitch or con game, comes from the Lord's Prayer, or rather the Latin version of 'Our Father,' *Paternoster*. *Canter* is what a horse does when it can't decide whether to walk or gallop – a kind of equine amble. It was shortened more than two centuries ago from *Canterbury gallop* (or *trot*, or *pace*) named for the gait at which pilgrims rode their horses toward the Kentish shrine of Thomas à Becket.

One of the oddest offshoots of liturgy is the word *placebo*, a pill or other medication that contains nothing therapeutic for the specific condition of the patient. In the 1400s, *placebo* was the common name for the Catholic vespers in the service for the dead. It is the future, first-person singular form of the Latin verb *placere*, 'to please,' and was the first word in the antiphon, or response, *Placebo Domino in regione vivorum*, or 'I shall please God in the land of the living.'

By the next century, common parlance had turned the church term into a caricature. To 'play placebo with' was to flatter or be servile toward someone, and soon the word by itself was a synonym for sycophant. Chaucer used it as a proper name for a toady in the *Merchant's Tale*.

This sense became obsolete in the mid-1600s, but the word was rejuvenated a century later by the medical profession to describe 'any medicine adapted more to please than benefit the patient.' To the doctors' amazement, the dummy dosage sometimes actually did some good, simply because the patient believed in it – the 'placebo effect,' it was called, and the phenomenon is still known by that term.

Antiphon, mentioned a couple of paragraphs ago, has evolved into another common word. This Greek word was *antefne* to the Anglo-Saxons, and later French influence changed it to *antempne* or *antemme*. Sometime after 1500, somebody decided it should have an *h* as in Anthony, and we ended up with *anthem*.

Meanwhile the word's meaning changed too. Originally the sung response in various church rites, it shifted to mean a song by the choir. By the mid-nineteenth century, the most common meaning was as a 'national anthem,' even though this was, and is, more precisely a hymn. Musicologist Carl Engel noted this in 1866, but added that 'It has, however, now been so generally adopted that it would be pedantic not to use it.'

But now, the language had no word for the ritual response. The solution was to resurrect *antiphon* in its original form – which appeals to the mumpsimus in me.

———————————   •   •   •   ———————————

In the beginning there were some words. Then came printed words, and the inevitable boo-boos. But who'd have thought that in Minnesota, they're boldly going where no Bible writers have gone before.

AND ON AN OFF DAY, GOD CREATED KLINGON

> The things that you're liable
> To read in the Bible –
> It ain't necessarily so.
> – Porgy and Bess, 1935

THE WORD FROM RED LAKE FALLS, MINNESOTA, WHICH IS ABOUT two hundred and fifty kilometres due south of Winnipeg, is that two scholars are hard at work writing the Klingon Authorized Version of the Bible – that is, the Bible translated into the language of the Klingons, warriors of the popular television series 'Star Trek.' Apparently it's based on a Klingon dictionary developed by linguist Marc Okrand and financed by Paramount Studios. One major snag in the Bible project was that Okrand's dictionary contained no word for God, since Klingons embrace no such concept. The translators solved this trekky question by using the Klingon word *joH'a*, or 'great lord.'

In case you missed the story, here's a sample of the gospel according to Klingon. The King James Version of John 3:16 begins, 'For God so loved the world ...' In Klingon that reads, 'toH qo' muSHa'pu'qu'mo' joH'a ...'

Now, I don't want to blow a shibboleth to Klingdom-come, but this whole business does raise a few quibbles in my normally forbearing mind. Why would anyone go to the enormous trouble of translating the Bible into an ersatz language spoken by fictional Godless aliens? Why, given the great difficulty anglophones have with apostrophes in their native tongue, would the creators of a new language strew them about like spermatozoa run amok? How do you pronounce 'pu'qu'mo'' and does it rhyme with anything in

English, or even pig Latin? And finally, are there prepositions in Klingon, and if so, are they okay to end sentences with?

There seems to be a great rage these days to translate the Bible into something or other. Heaven knows why, I assume. As somebody south of the Mason-Dixon line is reported to have said, 'If English was good enough for Jesus, it's good enough for me.'

Not long ago the African-American Family Press published *The Black Bible Chronicles*, a 'street' version of the Pentateuch, the first five books of the Old Testament. Impossible as it may seem to make 'thou shalt not kill' any shorter or plainer, this translation does it. 'Don't waste nobody,' it instructs. The seventh commandment removes any ambiguity there may be in the fancy word 'adultery.' 'Don't mess around with someone else's ol' man or ol' lady,' it warns.

The Genesis account of the flood also eschews antediluvian language. Here, a rather grumpy God says: 'I'm fed up, Noah, with what's happenin' round here. These folks ain't what's happenin' anymore, so I'm gonna do what I gotta do and end things once and for all. Man, I'm gonna blow the brothers clear outta the water.'

Over in Glasgow, Church of Scotland elder Jamie Stuart has also been rendering the Good Book into a modern Vulgate. His *Glasgow Gospel*, a fifty-nine-page version of the first four books of the New Testament published two years ago, is ripe with Glaswegian dialect. In the story of the 'Guid Samaritan,' one unkind stranger wants nothing to do with the helpless traveller who has been mugged and left naked in the road. Instead of offering aid, this callous commuter 'turns his heid, and gies him a nifty body swerve.' A more charitable sort from Samaria does give succour, however, and Jesus (according to Luke, according to Jamie Stuart) urges emulation of the worthy care-giver. 'Right then, Jimmy, jist you dae the same,' he advises.

The gospel description of the miracle of the loaves and fishes is done with proper Gorbals flabbergastation: 'Wid ye credit this? There wis ower five thoosan' men, weemen and weans takin' part in this muckle meal. Fair astonishin', so it wis!'

Unlike the Klingon caper, the *Black Bible Chronicles* and the *Glasgow Gospel* at least seem to serve some useful purpose – to make the Bible stories more understandable than the somewhat archaically worded versions still sanctioned by most churches. And they're not exactly breaking new ground. After all, the Old Testament was originally written in Hebrew and the New

Testament in Greek. They had to be translated into something for people not conversant with either of those ancient tongues. And sometimes things got lost – embarrassingly so – in the translation.

In a 1702 edition of the Bible, King David voiced a grievance familiar to writers throughout history. 'Printers have persecuted me without a cause,' he gripes to God in Psalm 119:161. Those early eighteenth-century readers who were aware that printers and printing were non-existent in David's time, must have puzzled over that. If they had checked another Bible, they would have found that the first word in the complaint should have been 'princes,' not 'printers,' though it was certainly the latter who bedevilled that 1702 edition. It was nicknamed the Printers' Bible, and it's one of many bibles that sport sobriquets based on typographical or other idiosyncrasies.

The Unrighteous Bible, printed in Cambridge in 1653, apparently didn't know right from wrong. In his letter to the Romans, Paul inveighed against promiscuity. 'Neither yield ye your members as instruments of right-eousness against sin,' he was quoted as saying, instead of the correct 'instruments of *un*righteousness.' Later, in I Corinthians, Paul was a printers' patsy again. 'Know ye not that the unrighteous shall inherit the Kingdom of God?' he asked. This time they got the unrighteous right, but omitted *not* before 'inherit.'

That little word *not* has probably caused printers more trouble than any other. It certainly gave Messrs Barker and Lucas problems in 1632. These London printers turned out a brand new Bible in which the seventh commandment read, 'Thou shalt commit adultery.' They were fined £300 for that lapse, and their work has gone down in Bibliana as the Wicked Bible.

Other biblical boo-boos are merely funny. The Ears to Ear Bible, 1810, could have been dubbed the Cockney Bible. Matthew 13.43 said: 'Who hath ears to ear, let him hear.' According to the Rebecca's Camels Bible, 1823, Genesis 24.61, 'Rebecca arose, and her camels ...' Make that *damsels*. In 1717 Oxford University's Clarendon Press issued a Bible in which the heading for Luke 20 was 'Parable of the Vinegar,' instead of *Vineyards*. That was not a vintage year for Oxford publishing.

All those nice people who allow others to go ahead of them in line-ups were beatified in the 1562 second edition of the Geneva Bible. In its version of the Sermon on the Mount, Christ was recorded as saying, 'Blessed are the placemakers.' An 1801 rendition was a little hard on whiners. An erratum has Jude 16 reading, 'These are the murderers, complainers, walking after their own lusts ...' 'Murderers' should have been *murmurers*. An 1806 Bible went one better than the competition by reporting a theretofore unrecorded miracle. Ezekiel 47.10 described a riverbank, and predicted, 'It shall come to pass that the fishes shall stand on it.' The correct word, *fishers*, takes the mystique out of it.

The To-Remain Bible, 1805, contained a real mind-bender. Galatians 4.29 said, 'he that was born after the flesh persecuted him that was born after the spirit to remain, even so it is now.' Those mystifying words *to remain* had been scribbled in the manuscript by an editor in reply to a proofreader's query as to whether the comma after 'spirit' ought to be there. The printers thought the editor's instruction was an insert, and there the words remained through two printings, while the comma went missing.

Not all the nicknamed bibles derive from typos. The Leda Bible was a 1572 edition that came all gussied up with elaborate woodcuts. At the head of the Epistle to the Hebrews was a gorgeous depiction of Jupiter, disguised as a swan, visiting the goddess Leda. Actually, he was doing more than visiting her, so this was not only a pagan ornamentation, but a pornographic one too.

The Geneva Bible was also called the Breeches Bible because it said Adam and Eve sewed fig-leaves together to make 'breeches,' an archaic meaning of which was 'loin-cloth.' In the King James version it's 'aprons.' Miles Coverdale's Bug Bible of 1535 gave Psalm 91:5 as: 'Thou shalt not nede to be afrayed for eny bugges by night.' *Bugges* meant bogymen. It was changed to 'terror' in later bibles, when bugs became insects – or flies in the ointment, like typographical errors, and other printers' devils.

————————————   •   •   •   ————————————

On All Hallows' Eve, ghosts, ghouls, and vile, ungodly apparitions tread the trembling earth in search of victims, or candy kisses. It's a good excuse to examine some of the skeletons in our etymological closet.

HAUNTING SHADES OF MEANING

From ghoulies and ghosties and long-leggety beasties
And things that go 'trick or treat' in the night,
Good Lord, deliver us!
                              – Cornish prayer, updated.

THE IRISH REPUTEDLY KNOW A LOT ABOUT WISPY, WONDROUS WEE folk, so I asked my friend Jack O'Lantern to ghost-write a column about Hallowe'en. This is what he scribbled.

Once (or more) upon a time, the heathen Celts of ancient Britain and Ireland celebrated the festival of Samhain – the end of summer – on October 31. The harvest was over, the herds were called in from pasture, and the dark and dead season was upon the land. It was a time when the souls of the departed revisited their homes. And it was a time when witches, goblins, and diverse demons in the form of black cats and fiendish fairies were most apt to be abroad.

The Celts lit huge bonfires on hilltops to frighten away the malignant travellers. It is well to remember that the first syllable in *bonfire* is not from the French for 'good,' as may be commonly suspected, but from *bone*, the chief ingredient of these pre-emptive pyres.

Ceremonies involved omens and auguries, purification and divination. Signs were sought in matters of love, marriage, prosperity, health, and death. Masquerading – often in the skins and heads of ritually slaughtered animals – was a popular form of celebration.

These orgies of mixed fear and frivolity continued until the middle of the ninth century AD. Until then, the Christians celebrated All Hallows' (or

Saints') Day on May 13. Rumour has it that Pope Gregory IV switched it to November 1 to supplant the pagan Samhain. If people were going to work themselves up over the dead, they might as well be dead martyrs and other late worthies. So the night of October 31 became known as All Hallows' Even, or Hallowe'en for short.

But Gregory's new broomstick did not sweep clean. Hallowe'en simply evolved into a secular celebration with a religious name, characterized by the vestigial antics of a passel of pagans. Among the gallivanting ghosties and short-leggety beasties who appear at your doorstep tonight, you'll find a few Ninja Turtles, clowns, and, no doubt, flocks of diminutive Blue Jay clones.

But the ghouls, ghosts, etc., will be there too. They've been a constant since the Dark Ages, even though the words themselves are younger and have undergone change. *Ghoul* is from Arabic *ghul*, an evil spirit thought to rob graves and do nasty things to human corpses. It's now used to describe anyone with slightly macabre tastes.

From their spelling, you might think that *ghoul* and *ghost* were etymologically related. But *ghost* is from an Old Teutonic word that spawned *gast* in Anglo-Saxon and *geist* in German. The phantom *h* was inserted by the first English printer, William Caxton, who spent many years in Belgium and was probably influenced by the Flemish *gheest*. We derived *ghastly* and *aghast* the same way.

Ghost has had many English meanings, including the human soul or spirit, the Third Person in the Trinity, an angel, the Devil, an apparition, various spurious images in electronics, and anonymous hacks like Yrs Truly.

Witch goes back a thousand years or more. In Old English it was either *wicca* or *wicce*, depending on the sex of the malefactor. *Goblin* is from the French *gobelin*, probably rooted in the Greek *kobaloi*, or wicked spirits invoked by rogues.

The generic jack-o'-lantern, as opposed to the proper name of the present scribe, probably came from the familiar name for a night-watchman. Using a pumpkin as the vehicle is a North American custom; in Scotland and northern England, turnips were used for the terrible talismans, and in the south they were made from mangel-wurzels.

Jack-o'-lanterns, with their traditional death-mask expressions (happy faces are a recent phenomenon) and their candles, provide a doubly symbolic reminder of times past. The fearsome façades conjure up the bogies and banshees that bedevilled our ancestors, and the guttering candles evoke the ancient bonfires that were meant to drive away the unwelcome wraiths.

Well, that should do the trick. As for the treat, I assume I get my usual 50 per cent cut – or else.

(signed) Your fiend, Jack.

———————————   •   •   •   ———————————

Several saintly monikers live on in everyday English. St Audrey, for instance, gave us 'tawdry' and St Mary of Bethlehem was corrupted to 'bedlam.' It's all divinely interesting.

EXAMINING RELICS OF THE SAINTS

ELSEWHERE WE POKED AROUND IN THE CREEPY CONCOMITANTS of Hallowe'en, or All Hallows' Eve. Lost in the garish grotesqueries of that celebration is the historical significance of the day after Hallowe'en – All Saints' Day. There's also some philological fun connected with some of those saints.

For about the first six hundred years of Christianity, the Church went busily about beatifying martyrs and others whose actions and lives embodied Christ's teachings. In most cases, a day of the year was assigned to honour these exemplars.

In 615 AD Pope Boniface IV (not to be confused with St Boniface [675–754], the English-born missionary who converted most of Germany, reformed the church in France, and founded a city near Winnipeg) saw two problems with this. First, there weren't enough days in the year. Second, the system might just have overlooked some deserving candidates. So Boniface dedicated May 13 to the Virgin Mary and all the Martyrs. Gregory III expanded the list of honourees to include 'all the just and perfect souls of God whose bodies rest throughout the world.'

One of these was Etheldreda – Audrey for short – founder and abbess of Ely Monastery in England. Twice married, but steadfastly chaste, she died of a throat tumour, which she regarded as God's condign retribution for her youthful passion for necklaces, which in those days were soft-wear, as the word *lace* might suggest.

Audrey became the most popular woman saint among Anglo-Saxon pilgrims, who flocked to her shrine wearing commemorative necklets called 'Seynt Audries chains.' At St Audrey's Day fairs, hucksters sold cheap, gaudy versions of these, and from that practice – combined with cavalier pronunciation – we got the word *tawdry*.

Mary Magdalene, named for her home town of Magdala on the shore of Galilee, wept copiously at Christ's tomb, and was rewarded by being the first witness to his resurrection. A late medieval form of her name was 'Maudeleyne,' from which we formed the adjective *maudlin*, meaning sloppily sentimental or sappily drunk.

Perhaps the best example of popular decanonization is St Valentine, a third-century martyr who met his end on February 14. No one knows why he became associated with romance and courtship, but it's thought there may be a connection with a folk belief that birds mated on that mid-February day. He has certainly become the unofficial patron saint of greeting-card companies.

Brigid of Ireland, said to have been baptized by St Patrick himself, was noted for her compassion. Legend has it that she changed her bath-water into beer to slake the thirst of unexpected visitors (presumably she herself changed into something decent). Her cult spread to England, where, among other things, St Bride's Church, Fleet Street, was named for her. Among the other things was St Bride's Well, beside which there was a hospital that was converted into a jail in the sixteenth century. For nearly three hundred years in England, *bridewell* was a synonym for 'prison.'

The London convent of St Mary of Bethlehem was converted after the Restoration into what was known, in those decidedly un-politically correct days, as a 'lunatic asylum.' From a slurred pronunciation of Bethlehem came *bedlam*, at first a generic word for mental hospital and eventually for cacophonous disarray.

St Pantalone, a fourth-century doctor and martyr, had a church named for him in Venice. Pantalone became a popular Venetian nickname, and was given to a tight-trousered buffoon character in a medieval stage comedy set in Venice. *Pantaloon* came into English as the word for a 'clown,' and *pantaloons* for 'trousers.' *Pantomime*, from the Greek *pantomimos*, 'imitator of all,' is an etymological cousin. But no matter who wears the *pants* or *panties* today, they can be traced all the way back to that early saint.

At the risk of sacrilege, we could say 'nuts' to the French martyr St Philibert, who gave his name to the *filbert*, which usually ripened around his day, August 22. But it's 'cheers' to St Benedict, an Italian hermit who was instrumental in transforming monasteries into centres of learning, agriculture, and hospitality, and who lent his name to one of the world's most famous liqueurs.

So, while All Hallows' Day belongs to all of the saints, some of the saints belong to all of us – at least in our everyday language.

———————————   •   •   •   ———————————

The adjectives 'happy' and 'merry' get vigorous workouts at Yuletide. But the rest of the year 'merry' lies dormant except for references to Robin Hood's men and various go-rounds.

WORKING JOLLY HARD AT CHRISTMAS

I F ADJECTIVES COULD GET TUCKERED OUT, THOSE BUSY LITTLE modifiers *merry* and *happy* should be profoundly pooped right about now. Like Santa's elves, these uncomplaining adjuncts have been doing their usual Yuletidy yeoman service for weeks now, putting in uncounted unpaid overtime, Saturdays and Sundays included, as the indispensable seasonal accessories of informal invocations involving Christmas and the imminent new year.

For *happy*, the annual year-end spasm of relentless rote work comes comparatively easier. It's younger than *merry*, and keeps in excellent condition all year with daily workouts at birthdays, anniversaries, assorted holidays, and certain periods loosely designated as 'hours' at sundry saloons. But *merry* is inactive to the point of inertia for much of the year – leading only the occasional chase, and adding jollity to a spring month and the odd 'go-round.'

Merry is by far the longer in the tooth, dating back to early Anglo-Saxon days, and before that to Greek and Indo-European. Its original meaning was 'short,' and the consensus is that the notion of 'shortening' or 'time flies when you're having fun' led to the later sense of causing or describing pleasure.

In Old English *merry* was spelled *myrge*, which also gave us our noun *mirth*, but not the agreeable *myrrh*, another word that gets a lot of unwonted exercise at this time of year. *Merry* could describe a thing or a sound ('this mirry gentil nychtingaill'), a condition or a place such as Merry England, the climate ('mery wedder'), someone's dress ('mery mantill'), or an amusing remark.

Merry was approaching its modern spelling by 1502, when William Atkynson wrote: 'Nothynge is more swete than is love – nothynge meryer.' But the early sense had little of the animated enjoyment the word now conveys. The more lively import developed around feasts and sporting events of the medieval period, and was well established by the time Shakespeare's Prince Arthur in *King John* (1595) says: 'I should be merry as the day is long.' Frequent use in descriptions of Robin Hood's band also added to its festive, roistering connotations.

English people spoke of a *merry mean* long before they referred to a *happy medium* as a desired condition between extremes. One extremity was 'making merry,' or getting drunk, as it's used in this chillingly matter-of-fact account by Narcissus Lutrell in 1681: 'Mr. Verdon, returning home pretty merry, took occasion to murder a man on the road.' Also at this coarse end of meaning was *merry-bout*, slang for 'sexual intercourse,' *merry-arsed* or 'wanton,' and *merry-begotten*, a crude term for a 'bastard.'

The first written record of *Merry Christmas* is from 1617, well before Charles Dickens popularized the expression in *A Christmas Carol* in 1843.

Happy, as it happens, comes from *hap*, which meant 'fortune,' 'lot,' or 'luck.' This sense is preserved in the negative *hapless* and, when you think of it, in our other modern words *happen, haphazard*, and *perhaps*. But early in its career *happy* put on a happy face, occurring more often in the sense of fortunate than merely fortuitous. At its best, it meant 'blest,' and the *happy land* was once a synonym for heaven.

By the mid-sixteenth century, the adjective settled into its present sig-nification of glad, pleased, content, or highly satisfied. In 1785, theologian William Paley gave it a fairly dour definition in his *Principles of Moral and Political Philosophy*: 'In strictness, any condition may be denominated happy, in which the amount or aggregate of pleasure exceeds that of pain.' Of course, he *was* talking about morals and politics in the same breath.

Happy has also had some pejorative flings. Like *merry*, it has been used colloquially for 'tipsy.' *Slap-happy* at various times has meant 'punch-drunk' or *happy-go-lucky* to the point of thoughtlessness. And you wouldn't welcome to your New Year's Eve party someone who was *trigger-happy*. When T.E. Lawrence in 1929 wrote, 'The camp is comfortable, and the airmen say it is a happy place,' he may have begat the abominable *happy camper*, an expression that for me causes many *happy returns* – Australian slang for vomiting.

———————————   •   •   •   ———————————

ONCE UPON A
HIPPOCRATIC OATH

In the old days, doctors were leeches, frantic didn't mean hectic, and hectic didn't mean hectic either – it meant feverish. Frantic meant mad. And as for lethargic, well, forget it.

OF LEECHES, LETHARGY, AND FEELING FRANTIC

W ELL, HOW WAS YOUR WEEK? A BIT HECTIC? FRANTIC, frenetic, frenzied? Verging on hysterical at times? Or did you just lie about since we last communed, indolent and lethargic?

If any of those adjectives applied to you during the past week, chances are you didn't need anything more potent than a mild sedative or a vitamin pill. But at one time, they signified symptoms that required more serious medical attention. You would, in all likelihood, have summoned a leech, which was once a quite polite term for 'doctor.'

If you complained of a hectic day at any time from the fourteenth to the nineteenth century, you would have indeed raised some eyebrows, and probably more sympathy than you would today. The adjective referred to a fever that was symptomatic of consumption or other wasting diseases, usually manifest by hot, dry skin and flushed cheeks. It was *etik* in Middle English, after the Old French *étique*, but eventually the spelling conformed more closely to the Greek root *hektikos*, 'habit-forming' or 'consumptive.'

By the nineteenth century *hectic* was used loosely to describe anything 'feverish,' and the concomitant flushed colouring was applied metaphorically as in the 'hectic red' leaves scattered in Shelley's *Ode to the West Wind*. The earliest known reference to the sense of frantic activity was Kipling's 1904 mention of a 'remarkably hectic day ahead of us' in *Traffics and Discoveries*.

Frantic, frenetic, and *frenzied* could all describe a stock exchange trading floor or rush hour on the parkway. Their common modern use belies a serious ancestry; they all descend from Greek *phrenitis*, 'head disease' or insanity. The adjectives derive from the noun *frenzy*, described in 1340 by Richard Hampole as 'a fantasie caused of trubblyng of the brayne.' *Frenzied* was formed on the English noun and *frenetic* followed the Greek pattern.

The latter sometimes came out as *phrentic*, which led to the corrupt *frantic*. All in their early use described a mental state characterized by raging violence, and all today are applied loosely to somewhat less deranged, but still fairly hectic, conditions.

Something outrageously funny today may be *hysterical*, but it wasn't always a laughing matter. It comes from the Greek *hystera*, 'womb' (as does *hysterectomy*), and originally referred to a nervous disorder attended by convulsions or fainting, also known as 'the vapours.' Because women were more susceptible to it than men, it was thought to stem from a disturbance in the uterus, hence the womb-based term. There is no prize here for guessing which sex dominated medical science at the time.

If all this talk of illness is making you *dolorous*, it may not help to know the word comes from the Latin *dolor*, 'grief' or 'pain.' The related verb *dolere* gave us *dolent* for 'sorrowful' or 'grieving,' as well as the opposite, *indolent*. In the seventeenth century, this was strictly a pathological term meaning 'causing no pain,' most often in connection with an 'indolent tumour.' But by the early 1700s, writers such as Addison and Steele were using it to describe people with an aversion to that painful pursuit called work.

In Greek mythology, a river in Hades was called Lethe. In the absence of saloons, dead souls drank from the Lethe in order to forget everything they said or did during their lives. Lethe is related to *lethargos*, 'forgetful,' and spawned our *lethargy*, a word that originally denoted a disease characterized by morbid drowsiness. It was often *lethal*, but this unrelated word is from Latin *letum*, 'death,' and probably got its *h* through erroneous association.

Which brings us to *leech*. In Old English, a *lyce* was a disgusting, but medically useful, blood-sucking worm. A physician was a *laece*, from an Old Scandinavian verb *läka*, 'to heal.' Because of the close professional association of the two, the former assimilated to the latter, and from about the year 1000 to late in the nineteenth century, one word – variously spelled *lech(e)*, *leach*, *leitch*, and *leech* – served to denote both the blood-letter and the bloodsucker. Even God and Christ were referred to in early writing as leeches, in the sense of 'healer.'

Presumably the pill-pushers and sawbones glommed onto a good PR firm about a century ago. Hardly anybody calls them leeches any more.

———————————   •   •   •   ———————————

The origins of the word 'treacle' lie in poisonous vipers and potions to treat snake-bite. These days the term is used to describe the work of Elton John, among other things.

THE LATEST TREACLE-DOWN THEORY

IN THE PAST YEAR, ABOUT THIRTY MILLION WORDS HAVE APPEARED IN the *Globe and Mail*, not counting ads, sports and stock market tables, movie and TV listings, crossword puzzles, horoscopes, and comics. In that ocean of typographical topicality, the word *treacle* was barely a drop. It appeared only six times, and in four of those instances it was in critical commentary, used figuratively to denote syrupy sentimentality – such as the book review that called Elton John 'the flamboyant master of treacle and tart.'

This is a pretty pejorative pass toward which *treacle* has trickled over the past couple of thousand years or so. Molasses-like, it has evolved from one unloved thing to quite another, and its serpentine journey is surely one of the oddest etymological odysseys in word history.

First there was the Greek *thêr*, for 'wild animal.' The diminutive *thêrion* was a 'poisonous viper.' Well in advance of the modern homoeopathic principle that like heals like, various viper bits were mixed up in potions used to treat snake-bites. These unguents, deemed most effective when they contained components of the actually culpable critter, were called *thêriakê*, which, for the technically minded, was the feminine singular form of the adjective formed on *thêrion*.

The Latin version was *theriaca*, and from there it slithered into all the Romanic languages. In French it became *triacle*, and it was this form that entered English in the fourteenth century. By that time, it meant any antidote or healing salve, the sense that has remained in all the Latin tongues except English. An interesting French spin-off is *triacleur*, which means 'charlatan,' 'quack,' 'mountebank,' or 'snake-oil salesman.' *Treacle-conner* was once an English slang equivalent.

The medicinal sense hung on for at least four centuries in our language. Around 1400, Walter Hylton wrote: 'This oynement is precyous, for it is tryacle made of venym to destroy venym.' And as late as 1804, a medical journal described a patented treacle, 'well-known for curing the venereal disease, rheumatism, scurvy, old-standing sores.'

For many years, Venice Treacle was held in the highest regard, but there was also Treacle of Genoa and of Flanders, not to mention Roman Treacle and London Treacle. For the less affluent there was Churl's, Countryman's, or Poor Man's treacle, whose chief and often sole ingredient was garlic.

Given the important role of the original snake-in-the-grass, Christian metaphors were inevitable. William Langland's *Piers Plowman* preached that 'treuthe telleth that love ys triacle for synne.' And Chaucer chimed in with 'Christ, that is to every harm triacle,' in the *Man of Law's Tale*.

Use of the word has helped to make collector's items of several early versions of the Bible. In Miles Coverdale's 1535 translation and the 'Bishops' Bible' of 1568, that old whiner Jeremiah laments the absence of *triacle* in Gilead, whereas in modern versions he bemoans the lack of *balm* thereat. These treasured oddities are known as 'Treacle Bibles.'

Balm, by the way, is related to *balsam*. Its adjective *balmy* went off on a tangent about three centuries ago, and is now used only in reference to breezes and air-heads.

Over the centuries, the *treacle* spelling gradually took hold, and the ointment evolved into a viperless draught, often sweetened to make it more palatable. The sense broadened to mean a sweet syrup of any kind, but usually that obtained in the process of refining sugar. It is virtually a synonym for *molasses* (from Latin *mel*, 'honey'), the word most commonly used for the sticky, dark fluid in the United States, although there is a technical difference between the two.

The latest stage in *treacle*'s evolution started sometime in the eighteenth century. Anything as sweet and gooey as this was naturally going to serve metaphoric duty, just as the word in earlier senses had. The earliest known example appeared in 1771, in Tobias Smollet's *The Expedition of Humphry Clinker*: 'He began to sweeten the natural acidity of his discourse with the treacle of compliment and commendation.'

While treacle puddings and treacle butter cakes are still popular in Britain, the word is nearly always used in its cloying, figurative sense on this continent. Who knows where this nomadic word will wander next? Maybe it will go full circle and end up making an asp of itself again.

•   •   •

A look at the lexicon of anatomy reveals that the human body is filled with animals and vegetables. For instance, our muscles are named after mice and parts of our eyes after lentils.

DISSECTING SOME
BODY LANGUAGE

THERE IS AN EXTRAVAGANT SIXTEENTH-CENTURY ENGRAVING depicting Andreas Vesalius, the Flemish father of modern anatomy, giving a lesson in an ornate, colonnaded operating theatre, surrounded by a press of curious colleagues and students. He is showing them the ins and outs, but mostly innards, of the human body, which are spilling from an enormous cavity in the belly of an erstwhile female person.

When I first saw this print – I was much younger and more mischievous then – I had an impulse to add voice balloons and rude comments to the already crowded scene. I happened upon it again recently and had a similar urge. Only this time the imagined dialogue was about anatomical terminology.

'Hey, get a load of that bone at the bottom of the spine,' crows one onlooker. 'It looks just like a cuckoo's bill.'

'Doesn't it though,' agrees Vesalius. 'I think we shall call it the *coccyx* [Greek for "cuckoo"].'

'And how about that little bundle of nerves sticking out just there,' says another, pointing daintily to a spot near the newly christened cuckoo's beak. 'Doesn't it look for all the world like a mare's tail?'

'You've got something there,' says the master. 'Let's name it the *cauda equina*.'

A sprint through the lexicon of anatomy suggests this embellished scene may not be as fanciful as it seems. The human body is an encyclopaedia of animals and vegetables, not to mention manufactured minerals of sundry shapes and purposes. The early dissectors certainly brought life to their nomenclature, even though they could not do likewise for the cadavers in their care.

Probably the best-known creature in the human make-up is the muscle. In Latin it's *musculus*, 'little mouse,' named not only because it looks like one but also because it was easier to say than 'a contractile fibrous band of tissue enabling movement in various parts of the body.'

Some muscles have other animal appellations. In the hands and feet we have *lumbricales*, or 'earth worms,' which help our fingers and toes move. In the thigh there's a hunk of web-shaped muscle called *pes anserinus*, or 'goose foot.' Higher up, in the intestines, there's a blind alley, *cæcum*, at one end of the *vermiform*, or 'worm-shaped,' appendix. And you know that flap just in front of your ear-hole, above the lobe? In the first century AD, Rufus of Ephesus, the first medical lexicographer, called it the *tragus*, or 'billy-goat,' because of the beard-like tuft of hairs often found on it. He also named the swirly part of the outer ear the *helix*, or 'swirly part.'

Namers waxed percussive over ear-bits. There's the ear-drum, or *tympanum*. In each ear there are three bones called *mallei*, 'hammers,' and one *incus*, or 'anvil,' to hit them on. The only way to escape the din is to run up or down one of three *scalae*, 'stairs' or 'ladders,' located nearby.

Hungry? Make some soup with your eye *lenses*, their name derived from the Latin word for 'lentil.' Swallow that fleshy glop at the back of your throat called the *uvula*, or 'small grape.' Or rustle up a mess of *fabellae*, 'little beans,' that you'll find in your knees. There's even a small pan there, the *patella* or 'knee-cap,' in which to cook them. For a condiment, reach for your hip-joint socket, called an *acetabulum*, or 'vinegar bottle.' Dinner music? Have someone tootle on your *tibia*, or 'flute.'

You may not have bats in your belfry, but you most certainly have nuts in your noodle. For more than two centuries, tonsils were known as 'almonds of the throat.' A group of nerve cells in the brain is known as the *amygdala*, Latin for 'almonds.' The brain also contains the shells of fruit stones, *putamen*; two sea monsters, or *hippocampi*; and a pine cone, the *pineal* gland. Both the brain and the heart have their own bellies, or *ventricles*.

You can't be inspired every day. Once Vesalius discovered a nondescript blood vessel in the face. He racked his brain for a metaphor. Nothing came. Finally one Adam's-apple polisher said: 'Why don't we call it the Vesalian vein?' And they did.

———————————   • • •   ———————————

Strictly speaking, one could attribute devil-may-care behaviour during the influenza season to forces beyond a mere mortal's control. Our ancestors used to get away with it – but only because they really believed it.

FEELING A BIT UNDER THE INFLUENCE?

WARNING: The following item contains an f-word. Astrological guidance is recommended.

THE F-WORD IN QUESTION IS THE FLU, THAT FOUL, ENFEEBLING bugbear of the winter months. What astrology has to do with it, we shall see.

Flu, or 'flu, as everyone knows, is short for *influenza*, a word that ascended to English language notoriety in the eighteenth century. In the spring of 1743, the *London Magazine* carried a chilling little news bulletin: 'News from Rome of a contagious Distemper raging there, call'd the *Influenza*.' The epidemic spread over all of Europe, and the word proved contagious throughout the English-speaking world. For all of the 1800s, it described not only the illness but also any prevalent craze or fad – like today's *mania*.

In its native Italy, *influenza* literally meant 'influence,' which literally meant 'flowing in.' It came from an Indo-European root *bhleu* (to swell up or overflow), from which *fluid, fluent, flux, affluent, fluctuate*, and *superfluous* also flowed. But *influenza* also signified a potent, unseen force, and it commonly referred to 'pull' in very high places.

As early as the fourth century the Latin ancestor *influxus* was often accompanied by the adjective *stellarum*, and this star-struck 'astral influence' denoted the flowing of an ethereal fluid from the heavens, which controlled the character, behaviour, and destiny of humans. The occult power was not always benevolent, and the Italian *influenza* came to mean the visitation of widespread sickness. It could be any affliction, such as the *influenza di catarro* or the *influenza di febbre scarlattina*. Such diseases could really take hold, so they were also called *la grippe*, another word imported by English with its spelling intact but its pronunciation anglicized.

At first, *influenza* in English referred to the specific disorder characterized by fever, muscle weakness, aches, and runny nose. It soon came to be applied loosely to any head cold, but the more serious version was sometimes specifically called an *influenza-cold*. Abbreviation to the one-syllable *flu*, with or without apostrophe, and sometimes even *flue*, occurred sometime in the early nineteenth century.

We already had the English word *influence*, which we cribbed from the French in the thirteenth century. Like its Italian cousin, it denoted both the literal 'inflow' of liquid and the figurative, mystical sense of astrological authority. Besides reflecting popular superstitions of the era, it was a handy excuse for misbehaviour. In a 1483 version of 'the devil made me do it,' William Caxton wrote of 'the synne whyche I have doon ageynst myn owne wylle and by the influence of the planette on whiche I was borne.' (Chronic cacographers may take comfort in noting that Caxton, sometimes known as the father of English spelling, spelled *which* two ways in one sentence.)

The down-to-earth Shakespeare saw through this hocus-pocus, however. In *King Lear*, Edmund, bastard son of the Earl of Gloster (Shakespeare's spelling was shaky at times too), scoffs: 'This is the elegant foppery of the world, that, when we are sick in fortune – often the surfeit of our own behaviour – we make guilty of our disasters the sun, the moon, and the stars; as if we were villains by necessity; fools by heavenly compulsion; knaves, thieves and treachers [as in treachery] by spherical predominance; drunkards, liars and adulterers by an enforced obedience of planetary influence.'

Fools, knaves, liars, and adulterers can no longer credibly claim extra-terrestrial grounds for their actions, but we still give drunks the benefit of the doubt when we say they're 'under the influence,' an expression coined about one hundred and fifty years ago.

Influence was beginning to take on its present, more mundane and secular meaning of 'sway' or 'control' by the mid-1600s. And we've known for some time that the flu doesn't come from the heavens, but from not eating our broccoli or not wearing our mittens. Personally, I don't believe in superstition. The fact that I haven't had the flu for years I attribute solely to clean living and pure thoughts. And if I touch wood, and keep my fingers crossed, I should make it through this winter too. After which I'll thank my lucky stars.

———————————   •   •   •   ———————————

Language is a living thing, of course, but the spontaneous practice of turning proper names directly into verbs is actually rather rare. Unless it's irresistible.

OF LYNCHING, BURKING, AND BOBBITTING

I REALLY, TRULY, HONESTLY TRIED TO STAY DETACHED FROM THE Bobbitt squabble – an affair so foul, I thought, so vulgar, gross, loathsome, and disgusting, that it probably wouldn't be getting all this attention if it wasn't so damned absorbing.

Wayne Bobbitt, I'm sure you'll recall, was at the wrong end of an act of violence in which Mrs Bobbitt, in vengeful retribution for a married life of abuse, cut off his penis with a kitchen knife.

It's been quite impossible to cut oneself off from it. Even if you don't read, watch, or listen to the news media, you can't avoid the ubiquitous small talk. Still, the possibility that this dreary dismemberment would become a 'Word Play' subject was far from my mind until I started hearing Bobbitt's name being used eponymously as a verb.

'I'm afraid I'm going to have to bobbitt this discussion,' I heard a colleague say to someone on the phone. Over by the water-cooler, someone else described a close call on the parkway. 'I was driving along, minding my own business,' she said, 'and suddenly this truck tries to bobbitt me.'

It's too early, of course, to know whether this trenchant new verb will take permanent root. But given the indecent exposure of the tacky trial, people a century from now may be lower-case *bobbitting* things left and right without thought to the word's grisly origin – in much the same way we 'sandwich' or 'boycott' things today.

If *bobbitt* does cut it as a household verb, it will join a very select company in our language. We have thousands of eponymous words and phrases – flowers, diseases, syndromes, machines, laws, and other things named after people who discovered, invented, or were afflicted by them. We also have a large number of eponymous verbs, usually formed by tacking an *-ize* on the end of a name, as in *pasteurize* and *galvanize*.

But only a handful of proper names have been verbified without additions or other amendments. *Sandwich* is one of the best known and most widely used. It appeared in the eighteenth century as a noun coined for compulsive gambler John Montagu, fourth earl of Sandwich, who ordered snacks of beef and bread so as not to interrupt his gaming for regular meals. It soon became a verb meaning to squeeze anything between two other things.

Capt. Charles Boycott managed the estates of the earl of Erne in County Mayo. In 1880 he ran afoul of the Irish Land League, a pressure group agitating for lower rents for tenant farmers. Boycott refused to give in, and at the urging of the league, his workers left him and suppliers cut him off. It was the first *boycott*, and the word was quickly adopted by other European languages, which didn't have a word for this activity either.

A number of these verbs arose, like *bobbitt*, from criminal proceedings. In the early nineteenth century two Irishmen, William Burke and William Hare, suffocated up to thirty people and sold their bodies to Edinburgh anatomists. They were eventually caught, and Burke's name became a verb for murder by suffocation. Over time the meaning broadened, and today in Britain to *burke* something is to stifle it or 'hush it up.'

A common verb meaning to summarily string someone up is the legacy of Capt. William Lynch, leader of a band of Virginia vigilantes at the time of the American Revolution. They dealt with lawless hooligans by inflicting 'such corporeal punishment as shall seem adequate to the crime committed or the damage sustained.' The sentence was often the rope, and such hasty hangings became known as *lynching*.

In the same neck of the woods is *guillotine*, after Dr Joseph Guillotin, who was not the inventor of the notorious French beheading machine, but the proponent – on humanitarian grounds – of its use.

Among the least known of these people verbs is my favourite, to *grimthorpe*. We owe it to Sir Edmund Beckett, first Lord Grimthorpe (1816–1905), whose restoration of St Alban's Cathedral in the 1870s attracted widespread criticism. His name became a verb meaning to restore an ancient building with a big budget but execrable taste.

I think that brings us full circle back to the egregious affair of Bobbitt, a name that may live in eponymy.

· · ·

Being beside yourself can be more than a figure of speech. It can be a moving, rapturous ecstasy. When it becomes an 'out-of-body experience,' it can also be pretty scary.

AT ODDS WITH AN ALTER EGO

FOR SOME OTHERWORLDLY REASON, I KEEP BUMPING INTO THE expression 'out-of-body-experience,' and it's driving me out of my mind – or maybe my mind out of me. I think I've had one, and it's kind of hard to describe. But for a start, yesterday I got up on the wrong side of the bed, and I also got up on the right side.

Now, I'm very often of two minds about things, but this was the first time I'd ever been of two *personae*. Talking to myself and getting an answer – sometimes even a heated argument – is nothing new. But being able to have a one-man *tête-à-tête* was a whole new unsettling experience.

Under the circumstances, I couldn't give this situation my undivided attention. I started to hem, and my alter ego began to haw. Not only did my right hand not know what my left was doing, there was another, equally independent pair at arm's length across the bed.

'What's going on here?' I ventured.

'You mean what's on-going here,' I replied. 'Nobody says "going on" any more.'

'This is no time for semantics,' I said.

'*Au contraire*,' said my opposite number. 'Semantics is what it's all about. You've been mucking with metaphors, dissecting similes, and fussing over other figures of speech too much lately. You've had your shoulder to the wheel, an ear to the ground, and your eye on the ball so much, you're coming apart at the seams – literally.'

On the horns of a double dilemma, me and my shadow padded into the bathroom to see if a splash of cold water would help. But the image in the mirror was decidedly two-faced, and when I spoke again, it was out of both sides of my mouth.

'I don't want to split hairs,' said my split image, barely disguising his amusement at this dubious *double-entendre*, 'but I think you've been dithering with words and phrases for so long you can no longer tell a trope from a trivet. In other words, your trolley has gone off the tracks. You're not all there – or all here, for that matter.'

'I think opinion is still divided on that,' I replied, not to be out-quipped by a clone. 'But I think you'll have to agree a lot of our colourful expressions involve figurative relocation of our anatomies or shifting bits of our bodies about. Why don't you get off your high horse and join me down in the dumps?'

'My heart goes out to you,' my counterpart countered, 'which is not the only excursion it's taken recently. Only the other day, my heart was in my mouth, then it sank. Then it leapt. Finally I lost it to this woman who looks like a facsimile of your betrothed.'

'You mean there's also two of my better half?' I gasped. 'If I'm not mistaken, that adds up to a better whole.' I could feel my skin creeping. My jaw dropped and my eyebrows rose. I didn't know whether to scream my head off or cry my eyes out. My head began to spin, my mind wandered, and I lost my tongue.

'Don't get your nose out of joint,' the disembodied doppelganger said. 'I can't stand it when you get your back up and fly off the handle. Let me give you a piece of my mind: Just let your hair down and let it all hang out before you go to pieces.'

I had the distinct impression that this disintegration was already well under way. I was torn between tearing a strip off this impertinent poltergeist and tearing him limb from limb. I was at the end of my tether – both ends, in fact. I gathered myself together, and asked, offhandedly, 'By the way, what line of work are you in?'

My twin didn't turn a hair. 'I'd give my eye-teeth to tell you, but my lips are sealed. Besides, I don't want to talk your ears off.'

But before evanescing through a wall, the chimerical chip off the old block handed me a business card. My eyes popped out of my head when I read, 'R. Cochrane, Ghost Writer.' My scalp crawled as I thought, 'He really was a dead ringer.'

I hear there's an 'out-of-body' chat category on the Internet, which I understand to be some sort of pit stop on the information superdragstrip. Apparently a lot of people are eager to have one of these extracorporeal excursions, judging by the frequently occurring requests for directions from electronic pen-pals.

I don't really see what all the fuss is about. Even apart from the above-described experience, I've been beside myself many times, and it's no big deal, except for the risk of a rather more distant and prolonged disembodiment than one might have bargained for. I suspect this may have happened to several acquaintances, who often tell me they're still trying to 'find' themselves.

The ancients had several words for it. One was ecstasy, from the Greek *ekstasis*, literally 'out of place,' but used by the Greeks to mean 'insane' or, at best, a bit befuddled. In late Greek the word took on the meaning of 'withdrawal of the soul from the body' in a mystic or prophetic trance.

When *ecstasy* emigrated to England in the fourteenth century (via Latin and French) it by no means carried today's sense of a condition devoutly to be wished. It denoted being 'beside oneself' with fear or anxiety. It still had this meaning in 1605 when the guilt-stricken Macbeth first complained of 'restless ecstasy' over the murder of King Duncan.

A few years later, when Milton wrote of sweet words that could 'dissolve me into ecstasies,' the word was obviously shifting toward its modern meaning of 'rapture,' 'transport,' 'emotion,' and 'excitement.'

Those words, too, contain a strong element of mental peregrination. The figurative meaning of *transported* – from the Latin, 'carried across' – is transparent. Movement is also clear in *emotion*, from Latin *emovere*, 'to move out.' *Excitement* got its marching orders from the Latin *exciere*, 'to set in motion.'

Someone who is *rapturous* is *rapt* in thoughts of lofty bliss. This was not always the case. Both words come from the Latin *rapere*, 'to seize and carry off,' which also gave us our words *rape, ravage, ravish,* and *rapacious*. In seventeenth-century English, *rapture* was a synonym for the violent *rape*, and *rapt* was the past tense of the verb. *Rapt* as a participial adjective has ameliorated 180 degrees in meaning.

Predatory birds such as eagles, hawks, buzzards, and owls are called *raptors* for no ecstatic reason; the noun connotes all the violence of its root. Similarly *ravenous*, contrary to appearance, has nothing to do with the black bird, but belongs to the same Latin *rapere* family. So does *ravine*, the geological scar that remains after erosion has 'seized and carried off' great amounts of earth.

You'd need a van to carry the huge number of words of the *transport* clan, all traceable to an Indo-European root *per,* to 'lead' or 'pass over.' They include *portal, porch, portage, export, support, portfolio,* and even *sport,* which is nothing but a clipped form of *disport,* meaning to divert or 'carry away' attention from serious matters. *Opportune* is from a Latin construction literally meaning to be 'carried toward the harbour.'

A Greek filter has given us *pore* and *emporium,* while Germanic influences have produced such words as *wayfarer, welfare, ferry,* and *ford.* The Indo-European root *meu,* to 'push away,' led to the Latin *movere,* the moving spirit behind a mountain of motive words. They range from the obvious *motor, automobile,* and *locomotive* to the somewhat disguised *promote* (move forward), *commotion* (intensive movement), *remote* (moved away), *moment* (movement of time), and *motif* (recurring or 'moving' theme).

An Indo-European root also caused *excitement* and its siblings. The ancient root was *kei,* 'to set in motion,' which it did to such words as *cite, incite, resuscitate* (literally, 'to again, from below, set moving'), and *solicitous* (thoroughly moved). The Greek offshoot from *kei* was *kinein,* from which we derived *cinema, kinetic,* and *telekinesis,* the alleged ability to move objects by will-power.

That seems to bring us back to the otherworldly, so I think I'll stop before I get, er, carried away.

———————————————   •   •   •   ———————————————

WORDS FOR
ALL SEASONS

An awful lot of our flora seem to have been named after fauna. There's catmint, dogwood, horehound, snapdragon, skunk-cabbage, horse chestnut, and cowslip. It's a menagerie out there.

BEASTS AMONG
THE BLOSSOMS

IT WAS THE SECOND MORN OF SUMMER, AND SPENT THUNDERHEADS retreated scowling before the laser thrusts of a burly, early-rising sun. In a North Toronto garden, back-lit pendants sagged glistening from blossom and bough, like carelessly applied lacquer. A soggy chiffon masterpiece of arachnoid art spanned a strategic flyway between the hydrangea and a crumbly cedar fence post, its resident architect perched idly awaiting an airborne breakfast.

Aside from one rumbustious robin, the distant thrum of freeway rubber, two chuddering, high-strung traffic helicopters, and the pulsing ululations of a fleeting ambulance, this moist and gleaming dawnscape was as mute as a mausoleum.

That's when the dandelion roared.

And the cockscomb crowed. The dogwoods and horehounds nipped and yapped at the catmint, and a surly snapdragon nonchalantly napalmed a sleepy skunk-cabbage. A horse chestnut whinnied fretfully and a low moody chorus emanated from the cowslips. This was no urban eden – it was a backyard animal farm!

Or so it seemed in the hallucinatory euphoria induced by a gladsome June morning, heightened by the fantasy and folklore enveloped in our names for things botanical. In some ancient orgy of zoomorphism, our forebears frivolously foisted faunal labels on floral species – thus, if not painting the tiger-lily, certainly animating it.

Folk etymology, that charming process of word formation that substitutes a familiar sound or idea for an archaic one ('rod-iron' for wrought iron), has worked overtime in our fields, forests, and gardens.

Samuel Johnson and a lot of others thought *gooseberry* derived naturally from the fact that its sauce commonly accompanied a roast goose; later etymologists discovered that it earlier had been called a *groseberry*, after the French *groseille*, and that there was nothing anserine in its background except wishful tinkering. Similarly, *asparagus* was, and often still is, called 'sparrow-grass,' and for nearly two centuries the *cucumber* bore the bovine name of 'cowcumber.'

Oxeye daisies were thought to resemble an ox's orb. With the *cowslip*, also known as marsh marigold, it's not so easy. In Old English, it was *cu-slyppe*, the second element meaning 'slime' or 'dung.' So the *cowslip* is known not by its appearance, but by the company it keeps.

The *dandelion* is a straightforward phonetic rendition of French *dent de lion*, or 'lion's tooth.' It's curious that, while we borrowed a French expression based on the weed's appearance, the French settled for a name related to quite another characteristic. The French word is *pissenlit*, which reflects the diuretic properties of the dandelion roots that used to be dried, ground up, and mixed with coffee. In fact, *pisse-abed* is given as an English alternative by John Gerarde in his 1597 *Herball, or General Historie of Plants*, and *pissabed salad*, containing dandelion greens, was once popular in the United States.

Snapdragons are so named because they fancifully resemble a dragon's jaws, and have also reminded people of a *lion's mouth* or *calf's snout* (the Latin name, *Antirrhinum*, means 'opposite the nose'). But folk etymology had a heavy hand in *horehound*. The 'hore' part is a spelling variant of *hoar*, or 'frost,' after the white downy pubescence that covers its stem and leaves. The other part in Old English was *hune*, the name of a plant, but eventually became *hound* because nobody knew what a *hune* was, and everybody was giving animal names to plants anyway.

In the field of grasses, the namers ran alphabetically amok. Here we have *adder, buffalo, canary, cocksfoot, eel, elephant, feather, horsetail, pony, sheep's, squirrel-tail, viper's, worm*, and *zebra grass*, and if we're unlucky, there may also be some pesky *pigweed, crab-grass, cat's ear*, or *chickweed*.

The medicinal *digitalis* is also known as *foxglove*. There is an easy link between 'glove' and the Latin botanical name, but no one has yet put a finger on the 'fox' connection. The lofty *lupine*, however, was named because it was erroneously thought to be 'wolf-like' (from Latin *lupus*, 'wolf') in de-vouring soil nutrients. In fact, as Martha Barnette points out in her splendid little book *A Garden of Words*, lupines are a soil enhancer.

Wolves lie doggo in other parts of the garden. Martha Barnette describes how the Greek wolf, *lukos*, lurks in a moss called *Lycopodium*, or 'wolf's foot,' and *Lycopersicum esculentum* is the botanical name for a 'juicy wolf-peach' – or what we call a tomato. A botanist with a fine sense of the ludicrous must have given the volatile puff-ball its classical name, *Lycoperdon*, which means 'wolf's fart.' Less menacing, and equally well disguised, is the gentle *columbine*, rooted in the Latin *columba*, or 'dove.' Turned upside-down, the columbine flower is said to resemble five pigeons huddled together.

Just for a *larkspur*, I was going to rave on about *toadstools, pussy willows, hen and chickens, hart's-tongue fern, stag's-horn moss*, and other denizens of my backyard bestiary, but I don't want the neighbours to think I'm as mad as a March *harebell*.

_____   •   •   •   _____

From the precocious little apricot to the ancient and ubiquitous apple, the delectable fruits of summer have sprouted many fig-ures of speech, legends, and folklore.

LIFE IS JUST A BOWL OF FRUIT METAPHORS

THE GREAT THING ABOUT THESE HIGH AND HANDSOME DAYS OF summer is the abundance of flesh – flesh of various shapes, expanses, and sun-kissed hues. Skin that is smooth and sleek, or soft and downy; tender and toothsome, yet firm and full of zesty youth. Succulent and sinful stuff you don't see in the winter. I'm talking, of course, about fresh, home-grown fruit. And the only thing more wonderful than their current plenitude is the astonishing history of some of their names.

The apricot (you say *AY-pri-cot*; I say *AH-pri-cot*) is a highly heterogeneous hybrid, etymologically speaking. The Romans called it *prunum* or *malum Armeniacum*, plum or apple of Armenia, because that's where they found it. Later they nicknamed it *praecoquum*, 'precocious one,' because it ripened in early summer.

The nickname passed into Greek as *praikokion*, then to Arabic *al* (the) *birquq*, to Spanish *albaricoque*, and eventually back to Italy as *albercocca* (now *albicocca*). Despite all this peregrination, the fruit didn't reach England until 1542 when Henry VIII's gardener brought some from Italy. He called them *abrecoks*.

In 1611, lexicographer John Minsheu logically but erroneously identified the word with the Latin *apricus*, 'sunny,' and Samuel Johnson swallowed this theory, stone and all, in his 1755 dictionary. On these authorities, the spelling changed to *apricock*, and later the ending altered in line with the French *abricot*.

The peach also does a good job of masking its name origin. Like the apricot, it's a native of China, and travelled westward to Persia before it was encountered by Europeans. The Greeks called it *melon Persikon*, and the Romans *malum Persicum*, both meaning 'Persian apple' (*apple*, both in the classical languages, and in English as late as the eighteenth century, was also a generic word for fruit).

The Latin term shortened to *persica* and this seed bore fruit in nearly every corner of Europe, producing the modern words *pesca* in Italian, *Pfirsich* in German, *persik* in Russian, *perzik* in Dutch, and *pêche* in French. From that menu, the medieval English naturally chose the French variety, as reflected by peach-lover Andrew Boorde, who published in 1542 *A Compendious Regyment or a Dyetary of Helth*: 'Peches doeth mollyfy the bely, and be colde.'

The cherry may also be a toponym, a word made from a geographical place. According to Pliny the Elder, the fruit was brought by the consul Lucullus from a Black Sea port called Cerasus. True story or no, the Latin word for cherry was *cerasus*. This evolved into the German *Kirsche*, and the Old Northern French *cherise*. The English mistook this for a plural, and coined the singular *cherry* to make up the perceived deficiency.

In Anglo-Saxon times the grape was sensibly called a *winberige*, or 'wineberry.' But since there weren't enough of them around England to really warrant a word, it became obsolete. When the need arose again in the 1200s, the English reached across the channel and plucked the Old French *grape*. That sounds straightforward enough until you discover that the French term originally had nothing to do with any fruit.

It was rooted in the old Germanic *krappon*, 'hook,' from which we also derive *grapple* and *grapnel*. This gave rise to the verb *graper*, meaning to gather bunches of grapes with a vine-hook. The noun *grape*, a back-formation from the verb, came to mean the bunch itself, and has broadened into the Modern French *grappe*, a bunch or cluster of anything.

If you've followed this so far, the rest should be a cinch. While we borrowed the French word for 'a bunch of grapes' to describe one grape, the French did the same with the Latin word for 'a bunch of grapes,' *racemus*. Only they spelled it *raisin*. We in turn took *raisin* to signify a dried grape. What the French did next is not recorded, but rumour has it that etymologists in both countries took to incoherent babbling.

If you're an old crab-apple or a prune who doesn't care a fig for fruity metaphors, you may want to skip the rest of this. And that'll be just peachy with me. The figurative senses of crab-apple and prune above are self-evident. But how did the fig become a symbol of the lowest level of concern, and the peach an emblem of excellence?

There's something quaintly Victorian about not 'caring a fig,' but it's unlikely that blue-nosed prudes would have uttered the phrase – certainly not if they'd suspected its origin.

Our word comes from the Old French *figue*, which grew from the Latin *ficus*. The Greeks called it *sukon*, from which we derived *sycamore* and, according to etymological folklore, *sycophant*. The Greeks allegedly forbade the exportation of highly prized Atticus figs, and the authorities paid inform-ants to hang around the shipping docks and blow the whistle if they saw any fig-shipping shenanigans. They were called *sycophants* – literally 'fig-showers.' The sense later developed into 'one who ingratiates himself with a superior,' a flatterer or toady.

It's possible, of course, that figs came to represent insignificance or worthlessness because they were cheap and plentiful in most Mediterranean countries. But *Oxford* and other dictionaries provide plausible evidence that the word derives from an indecent finger gesture known as 'showing (or giving) the fig,' which is quite another kettle of figs. In Greek, Latin, and most of the Romance languages, *fig* had another, impolite meaning, based on its fancied resemblance to the external female sex organs.

In most of these countries, and eventually in England, 'giving the fig' was to show utter contempt. Thus the gesture also symbolized another common *f* word, and 'figging' (as Shakespeare verbified it) probably evolved into 'not giving a fig,' or not caring less. And if not caring a fig is a disguised obscenity, it's also interesting that the expression is often accompanied by what may also be a bowdlerized gesture, a snap of the fingers, instead of an earlier, more explicitly lewd sign.

There is no such seamy side to peaches. They became a symbol of superlativeness simply because they were tasty, exotic, and an expensive luxury. The singular *peach* was used for anything special, sometimes a woman with a *peaches-and-cream* complexion.

In the early 1800s, plums became similarly super, for a like reason. The plum metaphor was probably reinforced by the happy discovery by a self-congratulatory Little Jack Horner. The adjective *plum*, as in a 'plum job,' may be a combination of this sense and a much earlier *plum* that meant 'plump.'

Bananas, though also foreign and rare, haven't done so well semantically. *Banana republic* is a contemptuous twentieth-century epithet for a Central American country, and *bananas* is an equally recent term for the Victorian *nuts*, which was a shorter way of saying 'off one's nut,' or head. *Banana belt*, oddly enough, is a Canadianism, first appearing in the *Medicine Hat News* in 1897, in reference to southerly regions of Canada with moderate climates, such as Lethbridge.

About seventy years ago, some stage director suggested that the extras in a crowd scene keep repeating the word *rhubarb* to create the impression of animated conversation or a hubbub. Before long, the word was being commonly used to mean an unruly disturbance. If the audience didn't like the scene, they might have given the cast the *raspberry*, a rude, derisive sound made by sticking the tongue out between closed lips and expelling air. The word is an abbreviation of *raspberry tart*, Cockney rhyming slang for *fart*, which the sound imitates.

Outside nursery rhymes and a well-known fairy tale, 'Cinderella,' the *pumpkin* contributed one of the least known – and, to me, funniest – words in the language. When the unpopular and womanizing Emperor Claudius died in AD 54, he was deified by the senate. This struck the philosopher Seneca as ludicrous, and he wrote a satire in which he called the emperor's apotheosis *apocolocyntosis*, or 'pumpkinification.'

Well, we've come to the mother of all fruits, the apple. I like to imagine that the earliest known apple metaphor, outside the Garden of Eden, was coined circa 9937 BC, and is exquisitely preserved in a sort of comic-strip cave drawing in the Mesopotamian Midlands. According to expert translation of the dialogue balloons in the various panels, it's clear that a prehistoric cave-couple are bickering at dinner.

She's complaining that he always gets home late, and he's upset because she can't make desserts the way Mother did. In the final panel, he has just sampled a fingerful from a steaming, lumpy mass, and it's evident from his bulging eyes and severely puckered lips that the concoction is not to his taste. It's also obvious that she's enjoying the spectacle, because she's saying, 'How do you like them apples?' This was not really a question, but a primitive form of rhetorical sarcasm.

The cave-hubby's sour reaction is understandable, given that early apples – or *abels*, as they were known in the ancient Indo-European tongues – were wild, small, and probably very bitter, like modern crab-apples. It's also possible the dubious dish contained anything from pomegranates to pistachio nuts, because *apple*, for many millennia and in many languages, including English, was both a specific name for apple and a generic word for fruit.

Because of its antiquity and ubiquity, the apple has sprouted more metaphors, legends, and folklore than any other fruit. In spite of proverbial advice to the contrary, the apple, not love of money, is the root of all evil. Its catalytic role in the original sin is well known, and the *Adam's apple*, a piece of the forbidden fruit stuck in all mortal throats, is a reminder that we are all rotten to the core. Some people think this story is just *apple-sauce*.

Apples have figured in other legendary strife. At a gathering of the Roman deities, Eris, a notorious mischief-maker, lobbed a golden apple (which was probably a quince) into a group that included Juno, Minerva, and Venus. The apple was inscribed, 'for the fairest,' and of course each of the three goddesses assumed it was for her. An unseemly squabble ensued, and the *apple of discord* became a symbol for any agent of dissension. It could just as easily have become the *quince of quibbling*, but it didn't.

The impish Eris was always *upsetting the apple-cart* like that, apparently trying to prove that *one rotten apple can spoil the whole barrel*. Her brother Ares was the god of war, which proves the *apple does not fall far from the tree*.

But it is a well-known certainty that *God made little apples*, so they can't all be bad. Taken in moderation – say, one a day – they are said to be quite salutary for the general population, and to reduce dramatically the medical profession's workload.

Long ago, doctors and others believed the optic pupil was a solid sphere, and they nicknamed it the *apple of the eye*. Since eyes were precious, the expression was extended to people or objects cherished by the beholder. It's possible to become such a darling through diligent *apple-polishing*, or toadying.

The origin of the expression *apple-pie order*, first recorded by Sir Walter Scott in 1839, is a mystery. It was once thought to be a corruption of the Old French *cap-à-pie*, 'armed from head to foot,' but there is no evidence that *cap-à-pie order* ever existed. The question is further vexed by the expression *apple-pie bed*, which describes a practical joke in which the bedsheets are folded, in un-*apple-pie order*, so that would-be snoozers can't get their legs fully stretched.

Several readers have asked where New York City's nickname, the *Big Apple*, came from. No one is sure, but in the 1930s there was a dance and, according to some sources, a Manhattan jazz club of the same name. Another theory is that musicians considered any city other than New York 'small apples,' but to get a Manhattan booking was to take a bite of the 'Big Apple.'

Eve and Adam did likewise, with the fruit of the Tree of Knowledge, and found that a little learning is a libidinous thing.

•   •   •

Egyptian astrologers identified two bad days each month. In Toronto, we identified several whole weeks of bad days and decided to call them November.

IT'S BEEN DISMAL AND DREARY, AS USUAL

I DON'T KNOW WHAT IT'S BEEN LIKE IN YOUR SCRUFF OF THE NECK of the woods lately, but here in the centre of the universe, a.k.a. North Toronto, it's been a pretty dismal, bleak, and dreary November. Maybe we can brighten things up a bit – although I seriously doubt it – by shedding some light on the extraordinary previous incarnations of those three adjectives, *dismal, bleak*, and *dreary*.

Nowadays we have plenty of things to divert ourselves with when the days are dismal. Four hundred years ago and more, dismalness had nothing to do with the weather or the season, and on dismal days it was best to do absolutely nothing.

In medieval English, *dismal* was a collective noun. It came from the Latin *dies mali*, literally 'bad days,' but carried the heavier connotation of evil, ill-omened, or potentially calamitous days. They were also known as the 'Egyptian Days' because they were originally identified by Egyptian astrologers, and there were two of them each month.

Eventually people began using *dismal* as an adjective, probably because it just sounded like one. They muttered about 'dismal days' even though the original word already contained this time element (just as most of us say 'the hoi polloi' even though *hoi* means 'the'). Then they started applying the adjective to other things, while still retaining the sense of sinister misfortune. In Shakespeare's *Henry VI*, the Prince of Wales proclaims, 'Now death shall stop his dismal threatening sound, and his ill-boding tongue no more shall speak.'

By the end of the Elizabethan era, *dismal* was losing its malignant mystique. People were using it to suggest anything merely gloomy, depressing, dark, or utterly cheerless. In the mid-nineteenth century, Thomas Carlyle coined the title 'dismal science' for economics. And in the late 1920s, a droopy-eared, sad-faced, and popular toy dog in England was called Dismal Desmond.

Things are not so black-and-white with *bleak*. Rather, they are more so, because *bleak* is virtually the same word as *bleach*, and originally meant 'pale,' or whitened by the sun.

It may be an outgrowth of *bleach* itself, or it may have developed from a Northern England word, *blake*, 'pallid' or 'wan.' This word was derived from the Old English *blac*, 'pale,' which in turn grew from the Indo-European root *bhel*, or 'shining white' (from which we also got *bald, blind, blink, blanket*, and, oddly enough, *black*). For centuries English speakers confused *blake* and *black*, and the confusion was compounded by the fact that both described a deficiency or lack of colour.

Blake passed into obsolescence in the sixteenth century, to be promptly replaced by *bleak*, which still meant 'pale,' but particularly denoted a lack of a healthy complexion. It was also used to describe an area barren of vegetation, and since such areas were usually cold, wind-swept, and dismal, the word eventually took on the meaning of chilly, gloomy, and dreary.

But if *bleak* meant 'colourless,' *dreary* in its earlier form was anything but. In Old English, *dreor* meant 'gore' or 'blood,' and its adjective *dreorig* was the forerunner of our *dreary*. Early on, the adjective took on the secondary meaning of 'cruel,' 'horrid,' or 'grievous,' but the connection with wounds persisted until after the Middle Ages. In 1590 Edmund Spenser wrote redundantly in the *Faerie Queene* about 'their drery wounds and bloody gore.'

At about the same time, the gory sense was ebbing, and soon a *dreary* person was a sad or doleful one, and *dreary* things were dismal, gloomy, or, at best, dull and uninteresting. In *Paradise Lost* (1667), John Milton sang of 'yon dreary plain ... the seat of desolation, void of light' and in 1884 the *Manchester Examiner* published this heartening report: 'The customs which made Sunday the dreariest day of the week are changing.'

That may be so. We can change customs. But we can't do anything with the weather but talk about it. And this November has been a month of cursed, bleached, and bloody Sundays.

• • •

There's a link between 'dome' and 'home' other than the Blue Jays hitting home runs in the SkyDome. It's all connected with the ancient word root 'dem,' which is also related to 'diamond,' which gets us back to baseball.

THERE'S NO PLACE LIKE DOME

B ETWEEN INNINGS OF A RECENT BLUE JAY TELECAST, I MUTE-zapped the commercials and idly toyed with the words *dome* and *home*. Would the beloved dome team win? How many dome runs would Joe Carter hit? Dome, sweet dome. Clever stuff like that.

Later, during an even quieter moment (John Olerud was beating out an inside-the-park single, so I had plenty of time), I repaired to my dictionary to see if there was any connection between those two similar words. There was. So here's the word: Be it ever so haughty, the SkyDome is just a humble home at heart.

The foundation for that homely pleasure dome is the prehistoric Indo-European root *dem*, or 'dwelling.' And from that modest beginning, an impressive array of English words grew, mainly in the rich humus of Latin. There, the ancient *dem* became *domus*, 'home' or 'house,' and sometime in the fifteenth century, English adapted it as *dome*, with the original meaning of 'home.'

But *dome* was always upwardly mobile. Influenced by French and Italian senses, it went from plain old house to a house of God, and then from a plain old church to a cathedral. It also described the rounded roof, or cupola, of a stately building, the vault of the sky (see SkyDome), a mountain, and, in slang, the human head. Perhaps to distinguish itself from these later meanings, the old *dome*stead got gussied up as *domicile*. The neo-Latin word *condominium*, for 'joint rule' or 'sovereignty,' came into the language in the early 1700s, and was adopted in the 1960s for co-owned apartments.

Dome-dwellers were, by definition, *domestic*, a word that first applied only to humans, but soon came to mean anything pertaining to the household, and eventually denoted 'indigenous' as opposed to 'foreign.' Most *domes* had at least one *domesticated* animal.

If you were a man around the Roman *domus*, you were a *dominus*, or lord and master. You were *dominant* in your domestic *domain*, maybe even *domineering, indomitable*, or *daunting*. If you were really self-important, you could be called a *major-domo*, a contemptuous term in English, but a serious VIP in Spain and Italy. In Portuguese *dom* became a title of respect toward upper-class men, as did *don* in Spain. The English university *don* dates from the seventeenth century, and was originally a term of sarcasm.

The feminine of *dominus* was *domina*, and from that came *dame, madam, Madonna*, and *duenna*.

The *predominant Dominus* was Jesus Christ, and for many years (AD, of course, or *anno domini*) Sunday was called the *Dominical*, or Lord's, Day. *Dominica*, or the Dominican Republic – a nation with SkyDome connections – was so-named because it was discovered on Sunday.

Experts agree *domino* derives from *dominus*, but nobody is sure how. In French it was an ecclesiastical hood or a mourning veil worn by women. Its earliest meaning in English was a loose cloak worn in conjunction with a mask at masquerades. Also uncertain is how the word came to describe the game with the rectangular pieces, although one theory is that some of the tiles resemble eyes peeking out of a black mask.

So much for the obvious ones.

A late Latin word for 'lordship' was *dominarium*, which became *dangier* in Old French and *danger* in English. If you were 'in danger' you were under the jurisdiction of a lord, or in his debt. Being in debt leaves you at peril or risk. Today, debt or no debt, *danger* means 'exposure to harm.'

A man's *dome* was his castle, and somewhere in the basement he probably had a guest room known as a *dungeon*. That's our spelling of the French *donjon*, a fairly grotesque outgrowth from the Latin *dominionem*, or 'ownership.' At some point, that Latin word took a more logical turn in the road and became *dominion*, a term with special significance for Canadians.

The Latin *adamanteus*, meaning invincible or 'hard as steel,' became our *adamant*. A corruption of this led to our word for an even harder substance, *diamond.* And with that discovery, I returned to the TV, and that diamond in the Dome.

———————————   •   •   •   ———————————

Entomologists and ordinary people have long been fascinated by this harbinger of summer. Etymologists have given former caterpillars much thought as well.

WHEN THE BUTTERFLIES FLUTTER BY

A S SURELY AS THE ROBIN IS A HERALD OF SPRING, THE BUTTERFLY is a certain sign of summer's arrival. And summer arrived in my garden this week, flaunted on the snowy, sun-dazzled wings of an early nectar-seeker.

Humans have always been fascinated by the butterfly, mainly because of its remarkable, magical metamorphosis from grub to gorgeous sylph. It may also involve life-style envy, for the adult lepidopteran is devoted to a single purpose. Its frequent floral visits are merely refuelling stops for the nectarean energy required for the exhausting airborne activity of perpetuating the species. Most of these winged sybarites probably aren't even aware that, in striving to produce baby butterflies, they are also helping to ensure another generation of buttercups.

Poets and minstrels have sung the butterfly's praises through the centuries, but the English writer John Gay feigned indifference.

> And what's a butterfly? At best
> He's but a caterpillar, drest.

Yes, but what a wardrobe! And what a challenge to our verbal powers to devise names that even begin to do justice to the chromatic phantasmagoria represented by the tens of thousands of different species of these gaudily clad caterpillars.

Colours naturally figure large in the common butterfly names. Aside from the ubiquitous Whites and Sulphurs (also called Brimstones), there is the

Pearly Marble, the Lustrous Copper, the Lilac-banded Longtail, the Wild Indigo Dusky Wing, and the Great Purple Hairstreak.

Emotion must have dictated the dubbing of the Sad Green Hairstreak, the Mournful Dusky Wing, and the Confused Cloudy. And perhaps it was an entomologically bent grammarian who saw the symbolism in the Semicolon, the Question Mark, and the Wandering Comma. But how can we account for the Tailless Swallowtail?

Of course, all of these creatures have boring but necessary Latin names, a practice credited to that great naturalist name-caller, Carl von Linné, alias Carolus Linnaeus, who also invented the umbrella name for the order, *lepidoptera*. It's a New Latin word from the Greek *lepido*, 'scale,' and *pteron*, 'wing,' and Linnaeus chose it for the flaky dust on the wings of butterflies and moths.

Moths are the shy members of the family, preferring to spend their waking hours at night, though still strangely attracted to flame and light. Perhaps they became self-conscious only after the Anglo-Saxons named them *moththes*, which was not only a mouthful but also meant 'maggots.' More palatable, perhaps, but much more mysterious, is the word *butterfly*.

Someone told me a long time ago that the word was a spoonerized *flutter-by*. This made a great deal of sense to me, and still would if it weren't for the total lack of evidence that the word ever existed. No, it was *butterfly*– or, rather, *buttorfleoge* – as early as AD 1000. To Chaucer in 1386 it was *boterflye*, and by Shakespeare's time it was as we now know it. There is no question it is made of the words *butter* and *fly*, but why butter?

American Alexander B. Klots, who was an entomologist, not an etymologist, said the name came from the yellow colour of the common European Sulphur, which also happens to be one of the commonest in the world. He noted that their pigment was formed by the uric acid wastes of their bodies.

The *Oxford English Dictionary* to date is unwilling to accept any theory, stating simply, 'The reason of the name is unknown [*sic*].' It does point out, however, that the Dutch *botervlieg* once had a synonym, *boterschijte*, and that one reputable Dutch philologist attributed this – rather unromantically, I think – to the colour of the insect's excrement.

Samuel Johnson's 1755 dictionary speculatively equated the name with early summer, when both butter and butterflies start churning.

My favourite story – and surely, to any reasonable person, the most plausible one – is that butterflies are really cunningly disguised fairies or goblins that *fly* around stealing *butter*. If I'm to accept that one of nature's most beautiful and graceful creatures evolves from a homely, hairy worm, I don't find butter-boosting fairies and goblins all that hard to swallow.

———————————   •   •   •   ———————————

A few of golf's rich and whimsical terms have rolled off the links over time. Now, even non-duffers can find themselves stymied or in the rough.

A LITTLE CRIBBING IS PAR FOR THE COURSE

S PRING IS JUST AROUND THE WEEKEND, AND ONE FINE DAY SOON, when the sap and the mercury are rising and the turf is firmer under-foot, thousands of usually rational Canadian adults will be found traipsing about variously shaped glades for the purpose of plopping dimpled spherules into ten-centimetre-deep holes in the ground.

In fewer words, the golfing season is nigh, except on the evergreen West Coast where, rumour has it, aficionados of the ancient pastime have this winter been able to harass the little white orb unhindered by any hibernal handicap.

I don't golf, but the St Andrew's Cross I bear in my genes harbours a residual respect for, if not envy of, the duffers across this dominion who even now are practising their stances, feigning mighty drives, and posturing im-probable putts in restive rehearsal for the serious fore!-play ahead.

You don't have to play the game to know that it possesses a terminology unrivalled by any sport in antiquity, mystery, and whimsy. It is popularly supposed that the word *golf* is a Scottish version of Dutch *kolf*, a club or stick used for various games, but the word appeared in English long before any related game was played in Holland. So mystery shrouds the name of the game itself.

Early on, national productivity suffered when the golf bug bit. In 1471 the Scottish parliament ruled that 'futbal and golf be abusit in tym cum-mnyng, & the buttis [targets] maid up, & schuting usit.' Translation: From now on, football and golf are out; archery is in. Golf was frivolous, but archery skills were needed for defence of the realm. The ban had little effect, however, and in the early sixteenth century, the Lord High Treasurer's accounts showed outlays by King James IV for 'golf clubbis and ballis.'

The game is played on a string of teeing grounds, fairways, greens, and assorted fiendish pitfalls. They are called *links*, a word that perversely has no connection to the segments of a chain, but stems from the Old English *hlinc*, a 'ridge' or 'hummock.' The word did not survive in standard English, but was preserved in Scottish, where its plural described undulating, treeless coastal land featuring dunes, coarse grass, and robust winds.

It wasn't good for much else, but it struck the Scots as excellent terrain for golf, and *links* now denotes any course, even if it's far from a salt breeze. All modern courses retain relics of the weather-beaten seaside links in the form of *bunkers*, a word of uncertain parentage, possibly related to *bench*. In fact, in Scottish it did signify a bench until Sir Walter Scott used it in 1824 to refer to 'a little sand-pit' on a moor.

Surprisingly few golf words have been naturalized in the common vocabulary. One is *stymie*, which means to 'thwart' or 'obstruct.' The old Scottish word *styme* meant the 'merest glimpse,' and from that developed *stymie*, a 'short-sighted, almost blind person.' By 1800 this word was being used for a golf-green situation in which one ball's 'view' of the cup was blocked by another.

The word *par*, meaning 'normal' or 'average,' is from the Latin *par*, meaning 'equal.' The expressions 'up to par' and 'below par' existed long before golf adopted the word about a century ago to signify the number of strokes a first-class player should need for a hole or a course. The modern metaphor 'par for the course' is a direct crib from golf, even though its hint of mediocrity belies the original notion of excellence in golf's *par*.

We sometimes 'tee up' or 'tee off' a meeting, and we can find ourselves figuratively 'in the rough' in many of life's endeavours, but we soon run out of golfing metaphors.

One fascinating part of the game that disappeared more than a half-century ago was the quaint array of club names – mashies, brassies, baffies, niblicks, spoons, and such. These proved too baffling to North Americans, whose sterile numeric system eventually prevailed over the ancient, antic nomenclature.

The *Globe*'s golf columnist, Lorne Rubenstein, recently wrote of a new move toward nicknames for clubs. But somehow 'Big Bertha' and the 'Divine

Nine' fail to evoke the sturdy, saline whiff of the windswept links where the game began.

———————————   •   •   •   ———————————

The Pit is not for the squeamish. In one corner, we have the pachysandra, which fights under the nom de guerre 'thick manliness'; in the other, the almost invincible periwinkle.

IT'S A JUNGLE OUT THERE

NOW THAT COCK-FIGHTING AND BEAR-BAITING ARE ILLEGAL, THE more bloodthirsty sports fans are forced to get their kicks from civilized mayhem like boxing, wrestling, or rush-hour at the Bloor-Yonge subway station. For variety, and a touch of pseudo-antiquity, US television now offers a show called 'American Gladiators,' in which fierce foepersons of both sexes assault fiendish obstacle courses and each other in costumes that reveal hyper-developed muscles and other biological mind-bogglers.

Call me kinky, but I like to indulge my sadistic side in my garden. Each day at dawn, while prying neighbours are still abed and the flying squads of the Herbaceous Humane Society are still gnawing on their vegetable-free breakfasts, I amble to the back forty (feet) and plunk myself in a folding chair beside a shady plot I call 'The Pit.'

Here I sit for a half-hour or so, just long enough to take in another pitched battle in the war of the ground covers. On this scorched earth, things don't just grow – they growl. And they fight, tooth and tendril. It's not a knock-down-drag-'em-out sort of thing. More like the Hundred Years' War in slow motion. But it's as ferocious as any struggle in history. Ground covers are naturally aggressive. They want *Lebensraum*, and they'll stop at nothing to get it. This, I've discovered, makes good spectator sport and appeals to man's basest instinct: sap-lust.

Two of my favourite militants are the pachysandra and the periwinkle.

The pachysandra, which also goes by the fearsome name of spurge, is by far the most virile and heroic of the wandering warriors. You would guess that from his name. The *pachys-* part is from the Greek *pakhus*, or 'thick' (as in the thick-skinned elephant, or pachyderm). The second part is from the Greek *andros*, 'male.' So the whole name – and here, the faint-hearted may want to cover their ears – means 'thick manliness,' derived from the plant's rather outsize reproductive organ known as the stamen.

The periwinkle is no pushover, despite its puny-sounding name. Its medieval spelling, *pervinke*, more faithfully reflects its Latin progenitor, as well as its bellicose tendencies. The Latin verb was *pervincere*, meaning 'to conquer completely.' The stem *vincere* also spawned such words as *victory*, *vanquish*, and *invincible*, as well as the name Vincent.

The periwinkle does not enjoy losing. So potent is his reputation that for a period during the fourteenth and fifteenth centuries, his name was a synonym for *ne plus ultra* – unsurpassable, paramount, the best, the champ. This was also the case in French; the dictionary compiled by Frédéric Gode-froy has this comment in Old French about a certain great vintage wine: 'De tous vins, ce est le pervenke.'

In earlier times, the periwinkle served as a trenchant symbol of utter vanquishment. It formed a garland that was placed on the heads of con-demned men on their way to execution. Hence the periwinkle's Italian name, *fiore di morte*.

The other flowers deplore this constant loosestrife – particularly the annuals, who feel life is too short for such brutal behaviour. One morning this week the pansies, who wouldn't hurt a fleabane, were out picketing with placards reading 'Make pollen, not war.' They kept a safe distance from the Pit, not because they're lily-livered but out of prudence, as their name, from French *pensée*, or 'thought,' would suggest.

The bleeding hearts are of course among the perennial protesters. And the pacifist primroses (unaware that their first syllable means 'prime,' not 'prudish,' and that they are not, in fact, roses) sit tut-tutting on the sidelines with the sweet williams and the forget-me-nots (whose family name is My-osotis, or 'mouse ear'). One time a tall blonde *Thunbergia*, called Susan, got a little too close to the action and suffered a black eye.

Me, I just sit there in a kind of euphorbia, enjoying my own dirty little secr ... hey! the periwinkle just got a vicious hemlock on the pachysandra! But I'm not holding my baby's breath. The season's still young, and there's a lot of ground to cover yet.

———————————   •   •   •   ———————————

The longbow, the crossbow, and their menacing missiles have given the language a rich range of terms related to the ancient art of aiming sharp, flighted objects at man, beast, and butt.

THE NUTS AND BOLTS OF ARCHERY

I T CAME TO ME THE OTHER DAY, LIKE A BOLT FROM THE BLUE, HOW indebted our language is to that ancient engine called the bow and arrow. Just for starters, had this handy missile machine never existed, I could not have involved that old bolt-from-the-blue cliché. And there are many more arrows in the quiver of verbal implements bequeathed to us by the noble practice of toxophily.

Toxophily is a fancy word for archery. It comes from the title character of Roger Ascham's *Toxophilus* (1545), and means 'lover of the bow.' The Greek word for bow was *toxon*, and the Greek word for arrow poison was *toxikon*, from which we derived our word *toxic*.

But in Ascham's day, the bow-and-arrow was already on its way out as a survival tool. In fact his book was largely a last-ditch defence of the longbow against the upstart crossbow, an early example of man's eternal quest for more efficiency in the art of killing.

While the bow-and-arrow was obsolete, except for sport, by the seventeenth century, no weapon will ever match its career longevity. It was invented, give or take a millennium, about fifty thousand years ago, and most historians rank its cultural importance with the discovery of fire and the development of speech.

The prehistoric Indo-European word root *arku* meant 'bow.' Through Germanic channels this became the Old English *earh* and eventually the modern *arrow*. That old *arku* in Latin became *arcus*, from which we obtained *arc*, *arch*, and *archery*. Since the ancient word for bow became arrow, our forebears had to have a word for the big bent stick, and they forged *boga* from the verb *bugan*, 'to bend.' That's how we got *bow*.

Another Indo-European root, *pleu*, 'to flow,' led to our verb *fly* and the noun *fledgling*, a young bird with new feathers. In French, this root became *flèche*, or 'arrow,' and the English eventually adapted this as *fletcher*, an 'arrow-maker.' Fletcher is also a family name, as are Archer, Bowman, and Arrowsmith.

A more common Old English word for arrow was *sceaft*, from the Latin *scapus*, 'stem.' This evolved into *shaft*, a utilitarian word that often became poetically metaphorized into sunbeams or bolts of lightning.

Which brings us back to the crossbow. Yet another Old English word for arrow was *bolt*, and for some reason this caught on with the crossbow crowd. Typically shorter and stouter, with a blunter, thicker head, it was also called a *quarrel*, from the Latin *quadrus*, 'square.' This is not related to the querulous *quarrel*, though it's best to avoid both.

The projectile *bolt* bred many offspring: the bolt of a door; the shaft-shaped bolt of cloth; the sturdy metal fastening bolt, along with its *nut*, formerly a projection on the crossbow used to hold the string until the trigger was pulled. A rifle bolt (1860) was not the bullet, but a rod for holding the cartridge in place. The poets liked *bolt* as well as *shaft*, and when Thomas Carlyle used 'a bolt out of the blue' in 1837, he was borrowing from the German *ein Blitz* (lightning flash) *aus blauem Himmel*, and the translation became fixed in English.

Bolt also has many verb senses – darting, springing, scoffing food, breaking away – all denoting the quick action of an arrow. The straightness of its flight also produced an adverb, as in 'bolt-upright.'

The earliest word for a target was *mark*, and it's easy to see how we derived expressions like *short of the mark*, *wide of the mark*, and *right on the mark*. A target for con men is an *easy mark*. In the early fifteenth century we adapted the French *but*, or 'goal,' added a *t*, and applied it to a mound of earth prepared as a practice target. The word survives today in the *butt*, or 'target,' of a practical joke. Archery buffs used to place a patch of white cloth on the *mark* or *butt* to represent the dead centre. From a distance, they naturally aimed somewhat above this *blank*, as it was called (from French *blanc*, 'white'). But up close, they pointed right at it, which led to the expression *point-blank*.

And with that, I'll bow out.

———————————   ·   ·   ·   ———————————

Skates and sleighs are probably more important symbols to Canadians than some of our more officially cherished emblems. Did anyone ever gasp with joy at finding a beaver under the Christmas tree?

THE SCHAKES AND SLEDES OF WINTER

I T PROBABLY SAYS SOMETHING ABOUT US CANADIANS THAT SO MANY of our important icons are images of sliding, skidding, or scudding over cold, slippery surfaces. Cornelius Krieghoff paintings, with their ubiquitous horse-drawn sleighs. William Kurelek's toque-topped shinny-players, frozen in mid-stride like the gelid prairie ponds beneath them. Kenneth Danby's defiant, death-masked goalie, mute and immutable. The crystal shrines called Maple Leaf Gardens and the Forum, their pristine pads carved and scarred by the blades of winter warriors or etched with the graceful serifs of more aesthetic skaters.

Sleighs and skates – objects of varying superstructures and of passengers even more diversiform, but uniformly dependent on thin strips of metal designed to conquer, accommodate, or even positively to enjoy winter's encrusted floor.

Skates and sleighs are probably more important symbols to Canadians than some of our officially cherished emblems. Did anyone ever gasp with joy at finding a maple leaf or a beaver under the Christmas tree? Did anyone ever dress hastily, bolt breakfast, and rush out to the nearest gradient or patch of ice to try out the shiny new Last Spike that Santa brought?

Sleighs and skates. They are the brittle warp and weft of Canada's hair-shirt fabric, the pith and marrow of our home and native land, the epitome of *eh*. And like a lot of us, or our forebears, both the technology and the terminology originally came from somewhere else.

Where I grew up, in the snow-belt city of London, Ontario, there were no 'sleds.' They were what dog-teams pulled somewhere up north. We had 'sleighs,' with names like Sno-King stencilled on their wooden platforms. The rest of the apparatus was steel, including a rudimentary steering mechanism, to which the tongue of every child, once and only once, became glued in the subzero temperature.

I can't recall reflecting, while careering down the proxy Alp of Lansdowne Avenue, on the derivation and odd spelling of *sleigh*. Now that I get more fun rummaging through dictionaries than rampaging down slippery slopes, I find that *sleigh* was originally a US word adapted from the Dutch *slee*. But sleighs were early on an indelible part of our own soulscape. This was noted in 1805 by Thomas Jefferson, who observed: 'The Canadian glows with delight in his sleigh and snow.'

The Dutch *slee* was a contracted form of *slede*, from which the English took the word *slead*, eventually settling for *sled*. The related Middle Dutch *sleedes* resulted in our *sledge*.

All of these slippery words are akin to the Nordic-rooted verb *slide*, which should surprise no one. Less known, perhaps, is that *sliding* predated *skating* as the word to describe skimming over ice on bladed boots. Jehan Palsgrave in 1530 noted, 'I have seen one in Hollande slyde as faste upon the yse as a bote doth when it is rowed.' Had he lived long enough to witness Rocket Richard, Gaetan Boucher, or Kurt Browning, he might have picked a speedier comparison.

Nearly two hundred years later, skating was still an oddity in English. In 1710, Jonathan Swift, in his *Journal to Stella*, described 'Rosamond's Pond full of the rabble sliding, and with Skates, if you know what those are.'

Whether Stella knew, or cared, is not recorded. But the history of *skate* has long fascinated word-lovers. We borrowed it from the Dutch *schaats*, for 'stilts' or 'skates,' and probably mingled it with the Old English *skatches*, 'stilts.' *Oxford* lets the trail die there, but A. Smythe Palmer, a nineteenth-century philologist, traced the Dutch *schaats* to the Low German *schake*, or 'shank.' This made sense to Palmer because, as he wrote, 'In early times a rude form of implement for sliding on the ice was constructed out of a shank-bone, tied on under the shoe.'

As evidence, he cited John Stow's 1603 *Survey of London*, which describes winter activity on the great frozen fen north of the city: 'Some tye bones to their feete ... and shoving themselves by a little picked staffe doe slide as swiftly as a birde flyeth in the air, or an arrow from a crossbow.'

I'll make no bones about it. With that soaring simile, Squire Stow was peering deep and straight into the future Canadian psyche.

•   •   •

On the Victoria Day weekend in most of this blooming land, people are busy in their gardens. They may appreciate a quick guide on how some of our basic earth-moving utensils got their names.

RAKE'S (AND SPADE'S) PROGRESS

I'M NOT GOING TO SPEAK WITH A FORKED TONGUE TODAY. I'M GOING to call a spade a spade, because we've got a hard row to hoe. So let's dig in and see what we can rake up.

It's the start of the Victoria Day weekend in most of Canada, traditional beginning of the serious home gardening season – except in Newfoundland, where it comes half-a-month later, if at all. Before we can plant the posies, we have some down and dirty work to do, and for this we need tools. And, in case you didn't twig from the preponderance of toolishness in the opening paragraph, that's what this is about.

Our tools will not be rusty or crusted with the desiccated residue of last autumn's muck because we all will have heeded the advice of John Fitzherbert's *A Newe Tracte or Tretyse Moost Profytable for All Husbande Men* (1523): 'A good husbande hath his forkes and rakes made redye in the wynter before.' That goes for a good wyfe too, or a syngle person, for that matter.

The names of many of our basic gardening utensils are rooted in Anglo-Saxon, as are many of the English language's most earthy words.

One of the oldest is *fork*, which was *forca* to our forebears. It was an agricultural implement to begin with, and wasn't used for eating – not in polite company, anyway – until the fifteenth century, influenced by the arrival of the fancy French *forche*. It has been applied to other utilitarian devices, such a tuning-fork, divining-rod, bicycle-forks, and the projection of a saddle.

In less felicitous settings, a *fork* has also been a weapon, a pickpocket, a spendthrift, a whipping-post, and a gallows. There can be a *fork* in a road, a river, and a tree, and the aforementioned *forked tongue* is named for the two-tined, venomous version you find on a viper.

A *pitchfork* was originally a *pickfork* or *pikefork*, and evolved to its present spelling through its association with pitching hay, sheaves, and other stuff. When it rained cats and dogs in the last century, you might also have heard someone say it was 'raining pitchforks perpendicular.'

When the Anglo-Saxons wanted to dig, they used either a *spadu* or a *scofl*. The first is our *spade*, a no-nonsense tool whose name, unlike *fork*, has not spread itself all over our vocabulary. Only a spade is called a spade (except for the playing-card, which comes from an Italian word for 'sword').

The expression 'to call a spade a spade,' meaning 'to speak bluntly,' goes back at least to first-century Greece, when Plutarch used it. Only he said 'boat' or 'basin,' the Greek word for which was similar enough to 'spade' to fool a later translator.

From *scofl* came *shovel*, as well as fifty-one spelling variants listed in the *Oxford English Dictionary*. Like *spade*, this close relative is not only a single-purpose utensil but also a unidimensional term, except for one modern adaptation. An old game called *shove-board*, in which a coin or disc was propelled along a polished surface by hand, inexplicably became known as *shovel-board* in the sixteenth century. Three centuries later it became *shuffle-board*, in which the propellant is a forked stick sometimes called a *shovel*.

The implement we know as a *rake* came from Old English *raca*, related to a slew of Germanic words meaning, oddly enough, 'shovel' or 'spade.' For some reason this tool became a proverbial symbol of thinness. 'And leene was his hors as is a rake' appears in the Prologue to *Canterbury Tales*. The simile eventually transferred to thin people themselves, who were called *rakes*.

Other people were called *rakes* too, but for a different reason. This word was originally *rake-hell*, denoting a blackguard, scoundrel, or utterly immoral, dissolute, and vile debauchee. Such a person was Brother Simkins in Christopher Anstey's *New Bath Guide* (1766). He gained his reputation by attending to 'cards and dances ev'ry day.'

The only member of our basic dirt-tool collection without an Anglo-Saxon pedigree is *hoe*, which we adapted from the French *houe*. They derived it from a Germanic verb for *hew*, but don't ask me how.

———————————   •   •   •   ———————————

A huge, early-winter storm in Southern Ontario had everybody searching for overblown words. There were lots of 'corkers,' plenty of 'doozies,' and even a 'lollapalooza' or two.

ONE HUMDINGER OF A SNOW JOB

THOSE OF YOU NOT PRIVILEGED TO LIVE SOMEWHERE ALONG THE north shore of Lake Ontario may have heard or read that Young Man Winter did a massive marshmallow job on the region a week ago. It was a snowstorm of Brobdingnagian dimensions. To say it blanketed the area (however apt that may be, since *blanket* derives from the French *blanc*, 'white') is like saying Santa Claus has five o'clock shadow. It was a lulu wrapped in a lollapalooza inside a humdinger, as southern Ontarians kept reminding each other incredulously as they hoisted more shovelfuls onto Himalayan-high heaps.

The stories are already legend. The storm of '92 was so bad, it's said, that the polar bears at the zoo refused to report for duty, and the snowy owls hooted in disbelief. The drifts on Toronto's waterfront were so deep that only the very tip of the CN Tower protruded, and the SkyDome is still missing. So stunning was this snowstorm that Mayor Mel Lastman of North York was at a loss for words.

Most of the words that were audible in this neck of the woods were of the hyperbolic sort mentioned above – the ones we reserve for truly uncommon occurrences.

'Wasn't that a dilly?' shouted my neighbour Lois as she mushed off to the corner store in a dog-sled ingeniously improvised from a plastic milk box, left-over spaghetti, and a tough tom-cat called Oreo. 'It sure was,' I replied, pausing to tighten the straps on the tennis racquets I had pressed into service as foot-gear. 'It was a real corker.'

The storm provided opportunities to get at long-neglected chores. I pointed the bricks around the top of my chimney, and pruned the uppermost branches of a forty-foot (dozen-meter) beech tree – both without the aid of a ladder.

Later, curled up before a *crackerjack* of a fire, I delved into the history of some of the wow-some words we use to describe doozies. Synonyms for 'the big one' seem to have two things in common: they can be used about things extraordinarily good or bad; and, almost invariably, no one knows how they began. This is understandable. When one is trying to outrun a tornado or a tidal wave and one exclaims, 'That's some bean-bruiser,' there is seldom an etymologist at hand to probe the word's provenance.

A *dilly* wasn't always a prodigy. In nineteenth-century Britain, it was a short form of *diligence*, the name for a stagecoach. It was also a familiar term for daffodil, and in this century it enjoyed a brief adjectival fling as a combination of *delightful* and *delicious*. In Australia a *dilly* person is both *daft* and *silly*. As a term for something surpassing remarkable, it arose in the United States early in this century.

A *corker* was once someone who put stoppers in bottles. The word became a slang term for something that put a stop to an argument. It figuratively expanded to anything that you 'couldn't get over,' then anything of stupefying effect.

Humdinger, American slang of unknown origin, is one of several superlatives based on sounds or images of speed or violence. *Ripper, whopper, whizbang, thumper, spanker, strapper, ripsnorter, knockout, piss-cutter, stunner*, and the Australian *big twist* are also in this category.

Australians also have *bonzer* or *bonza*, perhaps a mutilation of *bonanza*. But most of these words are from the United States, like *doozer* or *doozy*. The *Globe and Mail Style Book* and at least one other source say *doozy* derives from the magnificent Duesenberg, a powerful US car of the 1930s. But there are instances of its use as early as 1903, and most dictionaries feel *doozy* is a just a variant on the much earlier *daisy*, 'anything first-rate.'

The tamest of the wild bunch is *oner*, a unique person or thing. Its earliest print appearance in captivity is in Dickens's *Old Curiosity Shop*, published in 1840. Still a favourite with crossword puzzle setters, it was spelled *wunner* by several nineteenth-century authors. Likewise *beaut*, which seems to have sprung up independently in the United States, Australia, and New Zealand, has sometimes been rendered *bute*, reflecting its sound but masking its origin.

Which brings us to *lulu* and *lollapalooza*, American inventions that are not only *something else*, but also *something to write home about*. Or to write a column about after a *pip* of a storm.

—————————   •   •   •   —————————

It's official – winter's over, even if it may not seem like it. And while seasons change, the word 'spring' is one of the least altered – in meaning and spelling – in the language.

A SHORT SPRING SUMMARY

To begin at the beginning: It is spring ...
– Dylan Thomas, *Under Milk Wood*

THE BEGINNING IS A GOOD PLACE TO START, AND SPRING – WHICH makes its official reappearance today – has long symbolized rebirth and new beginnings. It has filled the hearts of poets, painters, and composers with rejuvenant inspiration, and caused the most soulless computer to re-boot spontaneously.

But the flowers that bloom in the spring, tra-la, cut no ice with most of the calendographers of history. Doggedly immune to spring fever, they have staunchly insisted – against all logic, all romantic instinct, and all physical evidence of rising sap and other vital juices – on pinning the year's beginning on a dark and dismal day at the beginning of January.

Mind you, mid-March in most parts of this dour dominion is not exactly a riot of bursting buds, heaving hyacinths, and unequivocal verdure. Only the most disoriented or restive robin redbreasts may be descried at this early date, and the seasonal debut of the hairy-chested Blue Jay (a rare, migratory, cud-chewing subspecies, indigenous to Toronto) is still more than a fortnight hence.

Thus, as the sun sidles equinoxiously across the earth's midsection, nudging the Northern Hemisphere into nominal spring and leaving the lower half to languish in autumn, we do not necessarily have cause to start yipping and panting like pubescent puppies.

The patently un-vernal equinox usually experienced in supra-tropical climes such as ours was neatly limned by Henry Van Dyke in an 1899 book called *Fisherman's Luck*: 'The first day of spring is one thing,' he said, 'and the first spring day is another.' The *Globe and Mail Style Book* adds this classically understated caution: 'In a country such as Canada, we should not make too much of the vernal equinox being the first day of spring.'

Nevertheless, spring is the start. French recognizes this in the word *printemps*, literally 'first season.' And whatever the meteorological reality outside your window right now, you know that the real spring, the fresh spring – the minty-green, recycled, environmentally amiable spring – cannot be far behind.

To find the source of *spring* you have to go far back in time. It may be one of the least changed words, in meaning and spelling, of any in our language. For a lark, Indo-European tribespersons would *sprengh* out from behind some prehistoric bush and yell 'boo!' (or *boogh*?), and from that *sprengh* sprang spring.

But the seasonal sense – just like the season itself, often – was a long time coming. Anglo-Saxons had the verb *springan*, 'to bound, leap or dart,' and the noun *sprynge*, a 'source or rising of water.' By the fifteenth century the sense had expanded to include a resilient metal device that powered evil contraptions called traps, catapults, and clocks, but later it found a more benign and practical application in shock absorbers for beds and vehicles.

The earliest chronological use of *spring* was to describe the sun's rising, and from the late fourteenth century until about 1600 *day-spring* was a synonym for 'dawn.' Burgeoning buds and blooms also suggested a connection with the nascent noun *spring*, and people began to speak of the 'spring of the leaf' and then 'spring of the year.' By the seventeenth century, spring, usually with a capital initial, had pushed aside the old *Lenten* as the preferred word for the first season. Until then Lent, still used for spring in German (*Lenz*), had done both spiritual and temporal duty. It grew from a Germanic root for 'long,' and in Anglo-Saxon it was *lencten*, which described the 'lengthening' of the days at this time of the year.

Such a fecund word as *spring* was bound to have many figurative offspring (to name one of them). So *spring* came to mean a 'flock of teal,' or the 'swelling of a cow's udder with milk.' On the Pacific Coast, a mature Chinook salmon is a 'spring.' You can have a spring in your step, or you could spring for the next round. You might have to spring a lock to spring someone from prison.

Come to think of it, you could quit wasting time here and get started on that spring cleaning. On the other hand, you could wait 'til spring, whenever that might be.

———————————————   •   •   •   ———————————————

ODDITIES
AND ENDITIES

A leisurely browse through the *Oxford English Dictionary* unearths enough tidbits to titillate a titivil, while a letter from a mayor offers a prayer for the return of missing 'ings.'

INDOLENT ETYMOLOGICAL PURSUITS

I T MAY NOT SHOCK YOU TO LEARN THAT ONE OF THE THINGS I LOVE doing in spare moments (I'll level with you; I enjoy it even more when there's something truly urgent needing my attention) is browsing through the *Oxford English Dictionary*. It's like poking around in your grand-parents' attic; you never know what quaint curiosity you'll find.

It was in such indolent pursuit that I stumbled on the word *quisquilious*. From the Latin *quisquiliae*, 'waste matter, refuse, rubbish,' this rare English adjective means garbage-like or trashy. Have the critics heard about this devilish descriptor?

Speaking of the devil, I also tripped over *titivil*, a demon who collects fragments of words carelessly dropped, skipped, or mumbled in the recitation of divine service, then hotfoots it back to hell to register them in each offender's logbook of moral lapses. The word is also used loosely (but not by anyone I know) as a term of reprobation for a scoundrel, knave, or villain, and especially a tattle-tale.

I immediately thought of Peter F. Trent, mayor of the City of West-mount, Quebec. Not that there is anything fiendish, knavish, or snitchy about Mr Trent — at least, that I know of. Implying that of someone who bears the honorific 'His Worship' might be blasphemous, or libellous, or at least rude. So I thought I should be very clear about this.

No, it's just that Mayor Trent wrote to me a while ago after I speculated here that there must be a limbo somewhere for lost bits of words — e.g., the missing letters in pop(ped)corn, ice(d) cream, and teen-age(d). 'Now,' wrote M. le maire, 'how about adjectival participles turned into nouns? It sets my teeth on edge every time I hear "fry pan, file cabinet, ship dates, cover letter, start date, race car, bomb run, and change room." '

The mayoral missive arrived at about the same time President-reject George Bush was announcing a 'no-fly' zone in Iraq, starting another tense wait game in the Middle East, not to mention making himself a laugh stock in the chief magisterial chambers of Westmount, Quebec.

The beating goes on. The chief status symbol of the horizontally mobile and obsessively communicative has already been truncated to 'cell phone,' possibly by those who have as much trouble getting their parts of speech around 'cellular' as they have with 'nukular.'

A person close to me thought all this was comical until I reminded her that, because she can't remember the difference between whipping-cream and whipped cream, she calls them both whip-cream.

In another excursion of self-distraction in the *OED*, I sat bolt upright at the discovery of *phallocrat*, denoting a man who 'argues his superiority over women because of his masculinity' – thus both begging the question and asking for trouble. This brought to mind a letter from Pamela Welbourn, of Peterborough, who came across the word *misopatry* in her local paper, used as the opposite of *misogyny*, or hatred of women.

'To me,' Ms Welbourn wrote, 'the word *misopatry* would mean hatred of my father. My biological training would lead me to suggest *misandry* as the correct term for hatred of men.' She said she could find neither in her dictionaries, and speculated whether 'no one felt the need for such a word until the present trend for using politically correct language emerged.'

Politically correct or not, *misandry* and Ms Welbourn have etymological correctness on their side. From Greek *miso*, 'hatred,' and *andr-*, 'man, male or husband,' it's listed in the *Oxford English Dictionary* and labelled a fad or 'nonce word,' although citations from 1946 and 1960 suggest a fairly longish nonce. It's also listed, without qualifying label, in *Webster's Third New International*.

I couldn't track down *misopatry*, but the *OED* offers *misopaterist* as a 'hater of the Fathers of the Christian Church.' Here are a few others that could come in handy these days: *misogamy*, 'hatred of marriage'; *misocapnist*, 'loather of tobacco smoke'; *misomath*, 'detester of mathematics'; *misopogon-istical*, 'of the hatred of beards'; *misogelastic*, 'hating laughter.'

We must fear more things than we hate; there are far more *-phobias* listed in the dictionary that there are *miso-*'s. Probably the best known of the latter is *misanthropy*, hatred of mankind, or of other humans. It likely owes at least some of its familiarity, even in English, to the great seventeenth-century satiric play *Le Misanthrope*, by Jean-Baptiste Poquelin, better known as Molière.

If there is such a word as *misomisoist* to describe someone who, like me, dislikes Japanese soybean paste, it's unknown to any dictionaries I consulted. And, before I jump from the fry pan into the fire line, I'm going to retire to my rock chair.

———————————   .   .   .   ———————————

There are many theories about the origin of one of the most universally used words. You can pick any one that seems okay to you, as long as it isn't totally 'out of karacter.'

A FEW OKAY THEORIES ... AUX QUAIS?

THOSE OF YOU WHO SOJOURN IN THE *GLOBE AND MAIL'S* 'Middle Kingdom' (a.k.a. the How-and-why-things-happen-page) may recall a headline that said, 'When it's not okay to say okay.' The story turned out to be a quiz about verbal and symbolic taboos in foreign countries, but did not address the question of 'when it's not okay to say okay.'

I'm not going to address it either. But I would like to try to unravel the multifarious theories about the origin of that ubiquitous word *okay*, OK?

All but a few far-out fringe theorists agree the word is American. But even Americans have disagreed on its importance. H.L. Mencken called it 'the most successful of Americanisms.' Margaret Nicholson, who published the Fowleresque *Dictionary of American-English Usage* in 1957, dubbed it 'a U.S. national disease.'

Good or bad, it has become one of the most universally used and understood words of any language. Right, then. Where did it come from?

Is *okay*'s ancestor the English word *hoacky*, a variant of *hockey*, meaning the end of the harvest or the drink-fest accompanying it? Does it come from the Finnish word *oikea* meaning 'correct'? How about the Choctaw *okeh*, for 'it is.' Or the Greek *ola kala*, for 'all is good.'

The trouble with these and some others coming right up is that the hypothesis stops there, with no attempt to explain the ascent from regional obscurity to planetary popularity. Or, as the *Oxford English Dictionary* puts it, they 'all lack any form of acceptable documentation.'

So where is it from? Is its source:

- The initials for 'outer keel' chalked on acceptable timbers by shipwrights?
- The homophonous 'aux quais' said to have been stencilled on casks of fine Puerto Rico rum selected for export (but why French in Puerto Rico?), or chalked on approved bales of cotton in Mississippi River ports? Or the sound-alike Aux Cayes, a Haitian port noted for its rum?
- The monogram of railway freight agent Obadiah Kelly, who signed bills of lading, or of Indian Chief Old Keokuk, who signed treaties? Or Otto Kaiser, the German-born American industrialist, who signed cheques?
- A short form of Orrins-Kendall crackers, favoured by Union troops in the US Civil War; or of 'zero killed,' part of a casualty report in World War I? Or letters indicating the rank of a German *Oberkommandant*?
- An anglicized version of the word for 'good' in Ewe, the West African language of many slaves taken to the United States, where they would have few occasions to use it.
- A variant of the agreeable Scottish exclamation 'och, aye!'

The answer is, none of the above. Nor any of a fistful of Latin, Scottish, Cockney, French, Norse-cum-Anglo-Saxon concoctions that have been put forward over the years.

The explanation now accepted by all etymologists and responsible dictionaries is the one expounded by Columbia University linguist Allen Walker Read in a series of articles in *American Speech* in 1963 and 1964. In the summer of 1838, he said, there was a fad among Boston and New York journalists that involved making up illiterate spellings of familiar phrases, then using abbreviations among themselves. One of these was 'oll korrect' or 'orl korrect,' the short form of which you have no doubt already divined.

As far as anyone has been able to discover, it first turned up in print in the Boston *Morning Post* on March 23, 1839, in an article by C.G. Greene. Within twelve months, *OK* was a commonplace expression of approval in the northeastern United States.

In March 1840 the *New York Era* reported the formation of the OK Club, a Tammany-sponsored group of Democratic activists. *OK* became the national democratic campaign rallying cry when President Martin Van Buren – nicknamed Old Kinderhook, after his New York State home town – was renominated.

His opponent, Gen. William Henry Harrison, also had a slogan –

'Tippecanoe and Tyler Too' – and his Whig supporters had fun twisting the *OK* into 'Out of Kash,' 'Out of Kredit,' and 'Out of Karacter.'

Old Kinderhook lost the election, and Harrison caught cold at his rainy inauguration and died after a month in office. But *OK* is still doing okay.

———————————   •   •   •   ———————————

The monarchy has given us all manner of odd titles, such as Yeoman of the Stirrup and Groom of the Crossbows, not to mention Knight Harbinger – or did you see that one coming?

HORSING AROUND WITH EQUERRIES

WITH ONE ROYAL MARRIAGE OFFICIALLY ON THE ROCKS AND A royal wedding in the offing, the Crown and its lexical trappings have been much in the news again of late. What better time to explore some of the mundane, magnificent, and sometimes mirthful expressions the monarchy has perpetuated for us.

Princess Anne's penchant for ponies is well known, and it seems to me that some horsy connection must be a prerequisite for suitors too. Royal Navy Commander Timothy Laurence, who is knotting the bowline with the princess this weekend, seems to fit the bill. He is an *equerry* to Her Majesty the Queen, and *equerry* has obvious equestrian links.

Or has it? Actually, the word is not an offspring of *equus*, Latin for 'horse,' even though that would be an instinctive guess. It is equine in both origin and current use, but its present spelling results from an etymological error. Two errors, in fact.

It comes from the Middle French *escurie* (now *écurie*), which was fashioned on the Latin *scuria*, or 'stable.' Somebody in the sixteenth century mixed it up with *escuyer*, the French word for *esquire*, so *esquiry* came into our language meaning royal stables, or the body of officers in charge of them. A century or so later, the error was compounded by the mistaken association with *equus*; so the *s* was dropped, and we ended up with *equerry*, with the stress on the first syllable rather than the second, as it should have been.

The word came to mean the household officer in charge of stables, and eventually broadened to mean an escort or protector of the monarch.

As Cdr. Laurence escorts Princess Anne down the bridal path, he may reflect that his temporary status as a bridegroom ('bride's attendant') is also saddled with equine and regal connotations. *Groom*, of uncertain origin, originally meant 'boy,' then 'man' or 'fellow.' By the mid-fourteenth century it commonly described a servant who looked after horses (a meaning it still has today), and before long it became part of many royal household titles, such as Groom of the Privy Chamber. At one time there was a Royal Groom-Porter, who regulated gaming within the court precincts, and made sure there were supplies of playing-cards and dice. There was also a derived slang word *grumporters*, for loaded dice.

If Cdr. Laurence plays his cards right, or has a stacked deck, he could become Marshal of the Court of Admiralty, in which case he would still be harnessed to a horse-related title. The word *marshal* comes from Old Teutonic, *marho*, 'horse' (from which we also get *mare*), and *skalko*, 'servant.' Its earliest English meaning was a 'blacksmith' or 'horse doctor.'

Monarchial menages have included many odd functionaries, including at one time or another Yeoman of the Stirrup, Sergeant of the Saucery, Groom of the Crossbows, Master of the Buckhounds, Lord Steward of the Green Cloth, Master of the Revels, and Hereditary Grand Almoner.

There are also some sleepers among our common household words that derive from royalty. One of them is *royalty*, originally a royal prerogative granted to an individual or company, and now the pittance paid to authors and composers.

Our word *coroner* comes from the Latin *corona*, or 'crown.' Once called *custos placitorum coronae* or 'guardian of the pleas of the crown,' this public officer now makes a living looking into untimely deaths. The adjective *coronary* was first used to describe crown-shaped vessels, ligaments, and nerves.

A *harbinger*, which was virtually the same as *harbourer*, at first meant a 'host' or 'innkeeper.' The word took on the meaning of someone sent ahead to secure lodgings for an army or royal entourage, and until 1846, the Royal Household had a Knight Harbinger. The 'going-ahead' sense eventually prevailed over the 'harbouring' sense, and the word now means simply a precursor or sign of something to come.

When we use the term *whipping-boy*, we should spare a thought for the word's human antecedent – a lad who was educated along with a young prince, and who got flogged whenever the prince did something naughty.

There were also whipping-girls for princesses, and I suppose there are some who would neutralize the terms to 'whipping-youngster.'

But I'll leave that horse for someone else to flog.

———————————   •   •   •   ———————————

Many inspired souls throughout history have invented words that live on to this day. But there are very few nouns whose origins can be pinpointed to an exact day. 'Scofflaw' is such a one.

A RICH HISTORY OF COINAGE

SEVENTY-TWO YEARS AGO, THE ENGLISH-SPEAKING WORLD AWOKE to the news of a blessed event – the birth of a new word.

One Delcevare King, a wealthy prohibitionist in Quincy, Massachusetts, had offered a prize of $200 to anyone who came up with a word that right-minded folk could wield against the 'lawless drinker to stab awake his conscience.' On January 16, 1924, the Boston *Herald* reported that, of 25,000 suggestions, the prize went to Henry Irving Shaw and Kate L. Butler, who had independently dreamed up *scofflaw*. A dozen years later, H.L. Mencken noted in *The American Language* that the newly coined word gained immediate and broad circulation, and 'survived until the collapse of Prohibition.'

In fact, it outlived both prohibition and Mencken. While not a full-fledged, everyday household word, *scofflaw* has been dragged back from the brink of obsolescence infrequently but regularly over the past decades to describe miscreants who don't pay parking-tickets or who find ways to avoid long-distance telephone charges. Twice in the last eighteen months it appeared in the *Globe and Mail* in reference to storekeepers who defied Sunday closing laws.

Scofflaw is one of only a handful of words in our vast language whose birth can be precisely pinned down to a person and a date. There are many others, not even counting arcane scientific words, commercial coinages such as nylon, Kodak, and Band-Aid, and pure nonsense words of the type Lewis Carroll specialized in, that can be safely attributed to individuals and at least approximate times.

One of the great early wordsmiths was the Roman statesman and orator Marcus Tullius Cicero (106–43 BC), who coined *qualitas*, from which we derived that wonderful word *quality* or 'whatness.' He also invented *indolentia*, forerunner to our *indolence*, which originally signified insensitivity to pain, but shifted in the eighteenth century toward the modern sense of aversion to work.

A notorious neologist was the Swiss physician and alchemist Theophrast von Hohenheim, who adopted the fanciful name Paracelsus ('beyond lofty'), and whose contemptuous contemporaries preferred 'Bombastus.' In a 1658 screed he cooked up names for the ethereal denizens of the four elements – earth, air, fire, and water. He dubbed the air spirit *sylph*, perhaps a blending of *sylvestris*, 'woods,' and *nympha*, 'bride.' Spirits of the earth, who supposedly swam through the formless primordial slime known as *chaos*, he called *gnomi*. Paracelsus' theories are extinct, but his *sylphs* and *gnomes* live on, in slightly and spritely modified senses.

At about the same time, Flemish chemist J.B. Van Helmont also brought some order out of *chaos*. From this Greek word for 'the nether abyss,' Van Helmont formed the word *gas*, possibly one of the most widely used 'made-up' words of all time.

In 1610 the Italian genius Galileo invented a tubular arrangement of lenses for making distant objects look closer, and called it a *perspicillum*. Prince Cesi, founder and head of the academy to which Galileo belonged, suggested the more apt *telescopium*, or 'distance-looker,' which has endured.

You didn't need a telescope to take in Robert Barker's 1787 invention called *La Nature à coup d'Oeil*. This was a landscape or other vast scene that unrolled before the spectator to show a 360-degree view. It could also be displayed on the inside surface of a cylindrical structure so that the viewer had to turn full-circle to view it. Barker later nicknamed the process *Panorama* (Greek 'all-view'), a word that now means any broad, impressive vista.

From the sublime to the nugiperous ('given to inventing trifles') we return to the twentieth century and to *blurb*, invented in 1907 by the noted neoterist Gelett Burgess. This word for a puff-piece on the back of a bookjacket originally was Burgess's surname for the buxom Miss Belinda Blurb, who graced a comic-book cover.

The prolific Burgess, who published a whole dictionary of his frivolous fabrications, is also credited with coining *bromide* to describe a person with a penchant for platitudes. Within a few years, the word became a commonplace, trite, even hackneyed synonym for *cliché*, and it is still used in that sense.

People are still scratching their heads over exactly what Edmund Spenser meant when, in *The Faerie Queene*, he used the theretofore unknown adjectives *blatant* and *elfin*. Context made John Milton's coinage *pandemonium* and John Dryden's *witticism* unambiguous to contemporary reads and equally clear to posterity.

Have I mentioned Shakespeare's monumental contribution of countless words, including *monumental* and *countless*? Well, maybe another time, and another whole book.

———————————   •   •   •   ———————————

Shuffling the letters in names or phrases to form other names or phrases has a long history. Pythagoras used to do it, as did Lewis Carroll, who created 'I lead, sir' from Disraeli.

BORN TO CHEER ACORNS*

HE EARLIEST KNOWN WRITTEN USE OF THE WORD SCRABBLE IS IN the first Book of Samuel in Thomas Matthew's 1537 Bible, relating how David feigned madness and 'scrabled on the dores of the gate.' It meant 'scrawl' or 'scribble' and still had that meaning three centuries later when Admiral W.H. Smyth, in his *Sailor's Word Book*, defined the noun *scrabble* as 'a badly written log.'

During the 1930s, when things were slow, architect Alfred Mosher Butts made scrabbling a game, in which players formed words from sets of mixed-up letters. In 1948 these letters-jumbled were granted letters-patent, and Scrabble went on to become one of the most popular word games ever.

I don't know whether Mr Butts, who died recently at the age of ninety-three, ever realized that the letters of his name could be rearranged to form 'rash of dumb letters.' I discovered it, aptly, with the help of Scrabble tiles, and its almost uncanny congruence made me wonder if there was something more to anagrams than coincidence.

It seems I wasn't the first to wonder. Some historians say that the sixth-century BC philosopher-mathematician Pythagoras, when he wasn't busy summing up the squares of the sides on right-angled triangles, liked to shuffle letters around to see if there was something profound in the results.

It's known that the fourth-century BC Greek poet Lycophon ingratiated himself with the rich and powerful by devising flattering anagrams of their names. There's also evidence that the Romans were fond of anagrams and other word games. One intriguing example was *rotas opera tenet arepo sator*,

---

* Anagram and family motto of Robertson Cochrane.

which loosely translates as 'God controls the universe.' When these words are stacked in a column, they read the same in all directions, which is clever but irrelevant. More pertinent, someone later found the words formed the anagram *retro Satana toto opere asper*, or 'Begone, Satan, cruel in all thy works!'

Anagrams were also favoured by the medieval Cabbalists, an esoteric group of Jewish scholars who believed in an oral tradition handed down directly from Moses, and who felt that letters of the alphabet had a spiritual quality. The fascination spread throughout literate Europe, and French King Louis XIII actually appointed a wordsmith, Thomas Billon, as Royal Anagrammist.

Some people got carried away. A story has it that André Pujon, an anagram fanatic, murdered somebody in Rion so that he could be hanged there, thus fulfilling the prophecy of his anagrammed name: *pendu à Rion* (the letters *i* and *j* were interchangeable). Anagrams were favoured for pseudonyms; Honoré de Balzac used only his first name and wrote under the noble title of Lord Rhoone, for example, and François Rabelais sometimes wrote under Alcofribas Nasier. Scientists often resorted to anagram handles in order to remain incognito until certain works were completed.

Forming anagrams of famous names became a fad in the nineteenth century. Someone divined 'we all make his praise' from the letters of William Shakespeare, and another wit turned Arthur Wellesley (duke of Wellington) into the retroactively prophetic 'truly he'll see war.' Lewis Carroll, who had lots of fun with words, created 'I lead, sir' from Disraeli, and forced Florence Nightingale to yield the enchanting 'flit on, cheering angel.'

Carroll thus set the standard for 'cognate anagrams' – shuffled letters that produce two words or phrases with a fitting or ironic relevance to each other, such as *astronomer* and *moon-starer*. He also gave the sport a twist when he challenged readers to make one word from 'new door.' There isn't one, and the answer was 'one word.' In the same spirit, *stifle* is an anagram of *itself*, but not of itself. For those who see mysticism in both letters and numbers, *eleven plus two* has the same letters as *twelve plus one*, and they both equal thirteen.

A *thermostat* can make *matters hot*, and a *schoolmaster* neatly transposes into *the classroom*. A *telegraph* is a *great help*, but satellite communications mean *it's now seen live* on *television news*. If newspaper *editorials* contain *adroit lies*, the editors may be forced to publish *retractions* (*to recant, sir*), and explain that the words were not meant to be *slanderous* or *done as slur*.

Well, it's time to bring this to a *grand finale* or – in other words, but the same letters – *a flaring end*.

There was a time when it wasn't cricket to call just any coloured flannel jacket a blazer. Things have become considerably more lax when it comes to jackets and slacks – not to mention frocks and smocks.

KEEPING OUT OF STEP IN FASHION

I LIKE TO KEEP UP ON MEN'S FASHIONS, NOT SO I CAN RUSH OUT AND replace my perfectly serviceable wardrobe every spring and fall, but just to monitor how far out of step I am with the latest styles – an out-of-stepness that can sometimes be measured in seven-league boots.

But some things don't go out of style, and one durable cog in the conventional man's gear is the blazer. I've donned one hundreds of times over the years, but it never dawned on me to wonder how such a drab, conservative item of apparel could have such an incandescent name.

Blazer, I discover, means just what it appears to mean, figuratively speaking. It first flickered to public attention in 1880 when a London *Times* article mentioned 'men in spotless flannels and club "blazers."' The quotation marks were a dead giveaway that a new word was a-kindle.

Within a decade, both the word and the jacket had become common currency, which prompted an indignant letter to the *Daily News*. 'In your article of today, you speak of a "striped red and black blazer,"' sniffed the reader. 'A blazer is the red flannel boating jacket worn by the Lady Margaret, St. John's College, Cambridge, Boat Club. When I was at Cambridge, it meant that and nothing else. It seems from your article that a blazer now means a coloured flannel jacket, whether for cricket, tennis, boating, or seaside wear.'

He was right. The blazer got its name from the fiery red colour of the jackets worn at Cambridge between 1850 and 1860. Maybe the word was also influenced by the coats-of-arms or crests often displayed on the breast. Another word for such a decoration is *blazon*.

The letter-writer's umbrage over popular expropriation and debasing of the word and/or the article would be even deeper if he knew that, a century later, the sporty jacket is rarely worn for sports of any kind. And, with a few gauche exceptions, it's coloured a most unpyrogenic navy blue.

Those 'spotless flannels' at Cambridge were probably white, or cream, but today's blazer is usually complemented by grey or tan trousers. The latter, once spelled *trowse* or *trouze*, was a singular noun from the Gaelic *triubhas*, or 'breeches.' Scottish *trews* is a variant. A 1639 book called *Conceits, Clinches, Flashes and Whimzies*, contained this adage: 'A jellous wife is like an Irish trouze, always close to a man's tayle.' The word became plural around 1600, and the second *r* was inserted because *trouzes* sounded to the English ear as though it had one.

Breeches is the oldest English word for men's pants, and is a curious example of a double plural. *Breec* was the Anglo-Saxon plural for *broc*, which was probably little more than a loin-cloth. The Middle English *breche* didn't look or sound like a plural, so people added an *s*. Dominant female spouses were said to 'wear the breeches' at least four centuries before the 'pants' version arose in the 1930s.

Trousers not belonging to a suit are often called *slacks,* and there's no hidden meaning here. The word comes from the adjective *slack*, which is rooted in the Latin *laxus*, 'loose, lax, or relaxed.' Even more casual are jeans, which have a longer history than one might expect. In the fifteenth century *jeane* was an adjective, meaning 'of Genoa,' and *jeane fustian* was a twilled cotton fabric soon shortened to *jean*. It was often used in trousers, and by the early 1900s, the plural *jeans* was commonly used to denote the pants themselves. *Blue jeans*, a term reflecting the most common colour of that item of apparel, dates from the mid-nineteenth century.

Denim was originally *serge de Nîmes*, after the French city. So when we speak of 'denim jeans' we're using what may be the only double eponym in the language. Two other words for the same clothing article, *dungarees* and *levis*, are also eponymous – the first from Dungri, a coarse calico named for a suburb of Bombay; the other from the famous jeans-maker Levi Strauss.

To someone who also keeps an eye on feminine fashion – from a polite distance, of course – women's wear is a welter of constantly fluctuating textures, tints, shapes, and hem-lengths. And that's just in the short term.

Over the centuries, the nomenclature and function of distaff duds have been even more confusing than their configurations. Lingerie (literally, 'made of linen'), once both dressy and highly visible, is now intimate and unseen, outside of Madonna concerts and the more brazen fashion shows. Petticoats also went outside-in. Smocks, on the other hand, spent their first eight hundred years of existence as unmentionables, but came out of the closet in the eighteenth century.

In a recent article, Joyce Carter, the *Globe and Mail*'s fashion reporter emeritus, said: 'the garment names are confusing because usage has perverted their meaning.' Indeed, some of the words have undergone a sort of terminological transvestism (from Latin *vestire*, 'to clothe'). Jumpers, petticoats, and frocks, for example, were once men-only apparel.

That jolly item known as a *jumper* – said to be poised for one of its periodic comebacks this fall and winter – is a prime example of a semantically shifted shift. This versatile vestment began as a *jup* or *jupe*, a loose tunic worn by both men and women in medieval days. The word mysteriously acquired an *m* by the seventeenth century, at which time it denoted either a short coat worn by Presbyterian ministers or a women's under-bodice used instead of corset-stays – a more incongruous pairing of simultaneous senses than which it is hard to imagine.

A century later, both the word and the apparel had lengthened. They were now a *jumper*, a loose jacket or shirt made of some stout material like canvas or coarse linen, worn by sailors and stevedores to protect their regular garb. Women reclaimed it in this century, but did nothing to clear up the confusion. In Britain, it's a woollen pullover, and on this continent, it's a one-piece, sleeveless 'pinafore dress.'

The pinafore, too, has flitted in and out of fashion, and with various significations. It was decidedly 'in' when Princess Anne married Captain Mark Phillips in 1973, and the *Times* reported that Lady Sarah Armstrong-Jones, a bridesmaid, 'wore a pinafore-dress.' It had come up in the world since two centuries earlier when it was merely a protective cloth or bib *pinned* on the front of (*afore*) children while eating.

The pinafore was nicknamed a *brat*, an even older Gaelic word for 'cloth' or 'apron.' Word experts think the modern word *brat*, for 'mischievous child,' comes from the same source, but have no written evidence of the transition from napkin to nipper.

The *frock* also has been fraught with multiple identities. Originally (circa 1350) it was an ankle-length, loose-sleeved robe worn by monks – hence the verb *defrock*. Two centuries later it was usually a women's dress, although a *frock-coat* commonly denoted a dressy, double-breasted, long-tailed jacket for gents. *Frock* came from the French *froc*, which may have originated in the Latin *floccus*, a tuft of wool or cotton.

The rhyming *smock* is one of the oldest words in the wardrobe. Before AD 1000, the Anglo-Saxons knew it as *smoc*, which they derived from a Germanic word for 'adornment.' It was then a women's undergarment, a 'chemise.' By the late 1800s, it described a women's or girls' dress, or a loose poncho worn by artists over their other clothes – much like the jumper before it jumped the gender gap.

Petticoat is easy to figure out from its early form. But the original *petty coat* was a small men's doublet, or an abbreviated coat of armour. By the mid-fifteenth century, it was a female dress, and before long had shrunk to only the lower half, or skirt, and then to an underskirt or half-slip, the meaning it retains today.

So there's no more coat in *petticoat*, and no pin in *pinafore*. But there never was a jump in *jumper* and, in case you wondered, nobody knows how the *jerkin* got its name. It may or may not be significant that it too was at one time strictly for men.

———————————   •   •   •   ———————————

Despite its somewhat awkward appearance, the word 'narcoterrorism' packs a lot of information into its five syllables, though you do need to be awake to get it.

DON'T BLAME YOUR LETHARGY ON PABLO

HAVING FELT MORE THAN NORMALLY LOGY AND LISTLESS OF LATE, I was stirred – though not to the point of actually sitting bolt upright – by the news that Colombian police had flushed out, then snuffed out, the world's most notorious 'narcoterrorist.'

Kidnapping, skyjacking, blackmail, political promising, and divers other extortive practices have become deplorably commonplace, but 'narcoterrorism' was a new one on me.

My first semi-somnolent reaction was that this phenomenon was somehow responsible for my recent unwonted lethargy. I sleepily surmised that narcoterrorism involved mass hypnosis through the already mind-numbing medium of television. But I haven't watched any soap operas, talk shows, or cable-ized legislative debates lately. I further speculated soporifically that it might be a heinous international plot to plant tsetse flies in everyone's ointment, or lace the world's water supplies with Nytol. But then, I never touch the stuff.

Curiosity got the better of comatosity. Wading deeper into the news reports, I eventually twigged that narcoterrorism was just some journalist's jaunty neologism for a multinational pharmaceutical corporation being run according to a somewhat Draconian code of business ethics. Pablo Escobar, the late CEO and narcoterrorist in question, was simply trying to diversify Colombia's traditional caffeine export base to include cocaine.

Narcoterrorism, for all its awkward appearance, does a fairly terse job of describing a rather hard-sell marketing technique, designed not only to monopolize supply and increase demand, but also to discourage meddling by would-be regulators. Just as with certain kitchenware and cosmetics, the only advertising is by word-of-mouth; the manufacturer is convinced, with good reason, that once you've tried the product, you're hooked.

That's a pretty big load for one word to carry, particularly one whose first two syllables originally connoted mere torpor. But it's an interesting illustration of how word meanings evolve with time and usage.

Some words start out with a limited and specific meaning, then broaden and generalize over the years. An excellent example of this is the word *thing*. In Old English, a *thing* was a public meeting; today it means anything, or any thing, at all – probably the most generalized noun in our vocabulary.

Other words go in the opposite direction, starting out with a broad meaning, then narrowing or specializing with time. An example is *deer*, which once described any four-footed animal, as distinguished from birds or fish, but now signifies only the Bambi or Rudolph kinds.

The prefix *narco* has done a bit of both. It's from the Greek *narke*, or 'numbness,' and in English has been around for more than six centuries, for most of that time related to sleep or drowsiness. It appeared in 1385 in Chaucer's *Legend of Good Women*, where 'narcotykis and opiis' are credited with inducing a 'longe slepe.'

The same Greek root sprouted the name *narcissus* for a plant with narcotic properties, as well as the flower's namesake, a mythical youth who was drugged by his own beauty. *Narcolepsy* entered the language in 1880 to describe a nervous disorder that causes attacks of somnolence.

By the early 1900s, the meaning of *narcotic* was expanding to include any mind-altering drug, not just those pushed by the sandman. But, outside of medical use, it was also narrowing to mean any such drug whose sale and use were illegal. These shifts irked the usually unruffled *Encyclopaedia Britannica*, which in 1974 said: 'Prejudice and ignorance have led to the labelling of all use of nonsanctioned drugs as addiction and of all drugs, when misused, as narcotics.'

The Beat Generation in the 1950s made a noun of the prefix *narco* and applied it to drug law enforcement officers. In the next decade it was shortened to *narc*. This was not to be – but probably was – confused with the older English slang word *nark*, for 'police spy or informer,' which was adapted in the nineteenth century from the Romany, or Gypsy, word *nak*, or 'nose.'

In Australia and New Zealand, *nark* was and is used for an annoying, obstructive, or quarrelsome person, or an unpleasant or vexatious incident. An English variant, *knark*, labels someone who is a ruthless, unfeeling person. Maybe we should make that *knarkoterrorism*.

━━━━━━━━━━━━━   •   •   •   ━━━━━━━━━━━━━

Confused use of prepositions is annoying, but it reflects a widespread puzzlement over these little parts of speech. Why do we have a change 'in' the weather but a change 'of' scenery?

UP WITH WHICH IT'S HARD TO PUT

IT'S OFTEN A SMALL STRAW THAT BREAKS THE CAMEL'S BACK, AND THE thing that snapped my serenity one recent morning was the puny preposition *for*. With a week left in the regular baseball schedule, the Toronto Blue Jays would miss the play-offs only if they lost all seven of their remaining games and the New York Yankees won all seven of theirs and then beat the Blue Jays in a tie-breaker. 'The odds for such a scenario,' said a story in the sports pages, 'are colossal.' Scenario-wise, I saw red and the air turned blue. 'Surely,' I sputtered, 'they mean the odds *against*.'

Prepositions – or the perverse use thereof – haven't always had that effect on me. Personal pronouns have been known to induce palpitations, and the feckless overuse of exclamation points has actually occasioned apoplectic interjections! But my attitude toward/as regards/about/concerning/with respect to/over/on/in terms of, and even anent, prepositions has largely been one of unstudied indifference.

Until a few years ago I had been oblivious to – or is it *of*? – the difficulty this small group of short words poses for many people. My first inkling of prepositional perplexity came from a headline in a small local newspaper, which said, 'Toronto group planning to erect statue for Dr King.' I deduced from the story that the doctor was Martin Luther King Jr, and that the statue in question was to be *of* him, not *for* him. The story added that the statue was to be 'a monument *of*' Dr King, not *to* him.

Alerted thus, I soon found the problem was not confined to small newspapers. A *Globe and Mail* travel story said visitors to Chicago could expect to be 'beset *upon*' by homeless beggars. A Reuters News Agency story reported that livestock were 'worth *between* $700 *to* $800 a head.'

A blurb at the bottom of a 'Facts and Arguments Page' column informed readers that the author 'writes *out of* London for the Observer News Service,' but did not say precisely where. A *Globe* sports story chided football commentator John Madden for misusing English, then noted that Madden 'has the tendency to reduce his otherwise astute sidekicks *into* mere straight men' – all of which reduced me into tears.

The puzzlement is not limited to modern ink-stained wretchedness. Essayist Sir Richard Steele wrote in 1712, 'I could not keep my eyes *off of* her' – a solecism that rasps many people who, on the other hand, see nothing wrong with its opposite, *onto*. Even earlier, in *The Tempest*, Shakespeare's Prospero observed, 'we are such stuff as dreams are made *on*.'

And English speakers were mangling prepositions long before Elizabethan times. The common word *about* began in Anglo-Saxon as *utan*, the locative (or positional) form of *ut*, or 'out.' Our forebears tacked on the prefix *be-*, meaning 'by,' to express the idea of 'out, but close by,' and eventually *be-utan* contracted to *butan*. Later generations felt the need for another prefix, so they added *on-*, creating the compound preposition *on-butan*, or 'on the outside of.' That prefix got shortened to *a-* (as it also did in *aboard*, *abed*, *a-hunting*, and *once-a-day*), and eventually our word *about* came about.

About has acquired about two dozen distinct meanings. Other prepositions have many more, and this versatility, coupled with capricious use in many idiomatic expressions, has led to a widespread befuddlement bordering on bedlam. Why do we have a change *in* the weather, but a change *of* scenery? Why is it okay to put people *up* for the night, but not nice to put them *down*?)

Teachers agree that these industrious but inconstant little parts of speech are the biggest stumbling-block for people learning English as a second language. But, judging by their willy-nilly deployment in everyday prose, they're no snap for native speakers either. It's getting harder to tell whether we're *out on* a tangent, or *off on* a limb. For generations, English users were bedevilled by an alleged rule against ending a sentence with a preposition. The problem now is that nobody seems sure which preposition to end a sentence at. Or with.

———————————   •   •   •   ———————————

'Dis' at the beginning of a word doesn't always convey a negative. Sometimes it's what's known as an intensifier. But please don't ask about 'dat.'

IF IT AIN'T BROKE, DON'T PREFIX IT

I WAS CONSOLATE, GUSTED, AND VERY MUCH MAYED TO DISCOVER I wasn't the only one who wondered if it's possible to be gruntled. Molly R. Hancock of Sudbury, Ontario, wrote to say the subject arose recently when a friend asked, 'How are you,' and she replied that she was a bit disgruntled. 'In that I am normally more gruntled than otherwise,' wrote Ms Hancock, 'we spent some interesting moments discussing what it might take to re-gruntle me.'

Actually, Ms Hancock may be credited in future lexicons as the coiner of the verb *regruntle*. In that case, she'd be in the company of P.G. Wodehouse, the first known user, in 1938, of the adjective *gruntled* to mean pleased or satisfied. This was an erroneous but irresistible back-formation of the verb *disgruntle*, which first appeared in the 1600s.

The mistake – or deliberate misuse – was to read the prefix *dis-* as a negative, as it is in most cases. The *dis-* in *disgruntle* is what's known as an intensifier, adding force or emphasis to the main word *gruntle*, which originally meant a little grunt by a pig or other animal, and later came to be a grumble or complaint by a human. *Disgruntle* was first used as a transitive verb in the seventeenth century, meaning to 'put into a bad mood,' but survives only in its past-participial form as an adjective.

Dis- does not often serve as an intensifier. One non-obsolete example is *disannul*, which doesn't mean to undo a previous annulment, but to annul it more completely, not to mention redundantly. Another is *disembowel*, which intensifies the already disgusting *embowel*.

In English, it's the little things that cause the most trouble. We've talked here about the difficulties many people have in sorting out prepositions. My guess is that prefixes pose as big a problem, especially to those for whom English is not a first language. For starters, a learner might ask, how is *especially* different from *specially*?

The common little prefix *in-* is fraught with ambiguity, and the most notorious example of this is the word *inflammable*. Does it mean 'capable of catching fire,' or the opposite?

At the beginning of a word, *in-* has two main, and mainly contradictory, functions. It reflects the directional sense of the adverb and preposition *in*, in such words as *invite, income, install*, and *insinuate*. It sometimes comes in disguise, depending on which letter it precedes, as in *illuminate, immerse*, and *irradiate*. In French, the old Latin *in-* became *en-*, so that we sometimes ended up with two versions of the same word, such as *inquire/enquire* and *insure/ensure*.

The second role of *in-* is to reverse the sense of the word to which it is attached. In the Germanic languages, this was expressed as *un-*, and this is the commonest negative prefix in English. But we also used Latin negative *in-* with a lot of Latin root words, for example, *innocent, insomnia, iniquity*. This contrary *in-* also travels incognito ('not known'), just like the other one, as in *illegal, immense* ('not measured'), and *irresolute*. Sometimes it shrinks to one letter, as in *i-gnorant*, and it is almost impossible to spot in *enemy* (from the Latin *in-imicus*, 'not a friend').

Inflammable belongs to the first group. It began with the verb *enflame* in the fourteenth century, meaning 'to set fire to.' Two centuries later, the prefix had changed to *in-*, and the adjective *inflammable* sprouted from the verb *inflame*. In the early 1800s, either in the belief that *inflammable* was a negative or the fear that it could be mistaken for one, people began to use the simple *flammable*. This would have solved the problem if the longer word had disappeared; but it didn't.

Around the turn of the century, somebody got the bright idea of tacking the unambiguous *non-* on either word. The possibility that some mistaken pedant will find a double negative in *non-inflammable* seems a small price to pay for greater clarity and, more important, physical safety. The best advice is, if you don't see a *non-*, assume the worst, and steer clear. Otherwise, you could end up somewhat short of combobulated, but more than a bit (dis)gruntled.

Perhaps the last people you'd expect to attempt to resuscitate obsolete adjectives are baseball managers. I was rather undisgruntled, then, when I read of a comment by Lou Piniella, manager of the Seattle Mariners, on the comparative decorum of Toronto Blue Jays fans. 'Toronto,' he said, 'is a pretty *ruly* place to watch a game.' It's always a pleasant surprise to find such a high degree of literacy among the sporting set – or anywhere else for that matter. On the other hand, maybe it was pure instinct that told Mr Piniella that, if there's an *unruly*, there's gotta be a *ruly*.

Whatever the case, he was right. *Ruly*, meaning 'law-abiding' or 'well-behaved,' dates back to about the year 1400. We'll have to assume he didn't mean the much older *ruly*, which stemmed from the verb *rue*, and signified 'regretful.' The orderly *ruly* disappeared into obsolescence around 1600, only to be revived in the nineteenth century by the likes of Benjamin Disraeli, who wrote of 'ruly soldiers.'

Oxford speculates that the modern revival was more likely a back-formation from the negative version, which has enjoyed uninterrupted currency for six centuries. Back-formations of this sort – from words that apparently have only a negative existence – are usually created for jocular effect, like *gruntled*.

Often the users of back-formed, or recoined, words are unaware that the creations once enjoyed lives of their own. A tidy example is *kempt*, shown in most abridged dictionaries as a back-formation of *unkempt*. But *kempt* originally was the past-participle of the Old English verb *cembian*, 'to comb,' and *unkempt* meant 'uncombed.' The latter was being used figuratively for 'untidy' as early as 1579 when Edmund Spenser wrote of his 'rugged and unkempt' rhymes. The old *kempt* slipped out of mainstream English, but is still used in some dialects in its original 'combed' sense, as is the verb *kemb* for 'comb.' *Kempt* meaning 'tidy or not unkempt' was revived by way of jocose back-formation in the 1920s.

An almost exact synonym for unkempt is *dishevelled*, but they did not always mean the same thing. The latter came into English in the early fifteenth century as *dishevely*, *dishevelee*, or even *discheiflee*, depending on which of Chaucer's stories you read. It was adapted from the Old French *deschevelé*, meaning 'stripped of hair, shaven, or bald.' There is no evidence that it ever denoted a literal lack of personal hair in English, but it was used to mean 'without coif or headdress.' But its most common sense is the one it retains today, that of disordered, unconfined hair, or what might be applied in the case of someone having 'a bad hair day.'

The non-negative form is, of course, *shevelled*, not to mention archaic and obsolete. It had some currency in the seventeenth and eighteenth centuries, but only as a short form for *dishevelled*. I have heard it used in revived form as a comical opposite of *dishevelled*, but I have also heard in the same sense *hevelled*, obviously used in ignorance of the *cheveux*, or 'hair,' in the French original.

When you're unkempt and dishevelled, you might feel almost *dismantled*, which was once no more than a simple opposite of *mantled*, wearing a cloak or robe. The negative form veered away from dress, and came to signify stripping a fort of its defensive equipment, or a ship of its rigging. It ended up meaning simply taking something apart, but I haven't heard of anyone trying to mantle Humpty-Dumpty.

Another good example of a revived positive stem is *couth*, which began its second incarnation a hundred years ago as a droll opposite of *uncouth*, or 'uncultured, ill-mannered.' In fact, *couth* was a common word more than a millennium ago. It was the past participle of the Old English verb *cunnan*, ancestor of our verb *can*. While we define *can* as 'being able to,' the Anglo-Saxon word had the subtly different sense of 'knowing how to.' Thus, the old *couth* meant 'known or familiar,' and it kept that meaning until it became totally unfamiliar – i.e., obsolete – in the sixteenth century.

Not surprisingly, *uncouth* originally meant 'unknown or unfamiliar.' This broadened to 'strange or alien,' then xenophobia finished the job by debasing the sense further to 'boorish, uncultured, ignorant, or ungainly.' The uncut *couth* never did disappear in Scotland. It survives in *couthie*, which has evolved from familiar to outright friendly, agreeable, pleasant, and genial. It also describes things that are snug or comfortable.

Did anyone pause awkwardly at the word *ungainly* above, and speculate on the possibility of *gainly*? Guess no more. Not only does the unaffixed *gainly* exist, it appears in many modern dictionaries, though usually labelled 'rare.' It means 'fit or graceful.'

There are two unrelated *gains* in English. The more common one is from the French *gagner*, 'to obtain, secure or win something.' The other is from Old Norse, whose adverb *gegn* shows up in such words as *against*, *again*, and *gainsay*. The related Old Norse verb *gegna*, meaning 'to come against,' or meet, produced the English verb *gain*, which meant the same thing, but also signified to be 'meet,' an archaic word for 'fitting or appropriate.' This verb has been long obsolete, but its offspring *ungainly* is still alive and lurching.

At one time, a precise synonym for *ungainly* was *unwieldy*. In the fourteenth century, *wieldy* meant 'easy-moving,' or agile, nimble. The negative *unwieldy* is today usually reserved for things, not humans, that are cumbersome or difficult to move or manage, but is sometimes used for people, especially children, who are recalcitrant, defiant, or indocile. This puts it in the same ballpark as unruly – although not the rigorously ruly place where Toronto baseball fans politely and rulily gather.

———————————————   •   •   •   ———————————————

At one time, 'virtual' simply meant 'full of virtue,' as in 'A virtual woman is a crown to her husband.' But first, let's talk about something real, like virgins, viragos, and werewolves.

VIRTUAL VIRTUE: IT'S A MIRACLE!

YOU PROBABLY SAW THE STORY IN LAST WEEKEND'S *GLOBE* ABOUT 'virtual reality,' the electronic wizardry that simulates intangible palpability, or lifelike artificiality, or something like that.

The truly amazing thing is that somebody out there knows the difference between 'virtual' and 'literal' – a distinction that seems to be getting pretty fuzzy these days. And this virtually hands us on a plate the excuse to explore the vagaries of the word *virtual*, and its predecessors and kin.

It all started on April 1 in the year 4984 BC, when a shaggy, club-toting guy made a pass at a demure damsel in a cave bar. She brushed him off, saying, 'Take a hike, weirdo.' But he thought she said 'wiro.' He rather liked the sound of it, so he introduced himself that way for the rest of his short and unfulfilled life. The word caught on, and *wiro* became an accepted Indo-European word for 'man,' alongside another short word, which was, coincidentally enough, *man*.

Invading Europeans brought both words with them to England, but the former, rendered *wer* in Old English, survives today only in the imaginary *werewolf*. In disguised form it also lurks in a much more common modern word. We derived it from a Germanic blend *wer-ald*, meaning 'age of man,' and we call it *world*.

Meanwhile, back in Europe around 1000 BC, in a village set among seven hills on the banks of the Tiber River, people had changed the old Indo-European root to *vir*, although they still pronounced the first letter as a *w*. The area was known as Latium, and it would develop into a mighty city, to which all roads led. Like most cities, it was not built in a day, but for some reason it became famous for this unremarkable fact.

The Latin word for man-like was *virilis*, which at a later time in another place became *virile*. In fifteenth-century English this meant 'strong and forceful.' It was often applied to women who displayed positive man-like virtues. By the same token, unvirile men were described as effeminate.

The gender gap was opening long before that, however. According to an early Latin Bible, Adam's first words to his newly created mate were not 'Madam, I'm Adam,' but something like, 'Me *vir*, you *virago*.' This word, meaning 'made from man,' was reportedly Eve's name before she sinned. It didn't make a pat palindrome, but it did give us a word to describe a bold, heroic woman, and specifically denoted an Amazon warrior. Not everyone liked these characteristics in a woman, so the word degenerated to mean a 'shrew' or a 'scold,' its present meaning.

Etymologists have been unable to find a clear link between *virago* and *virgin*, although Eric Partridge speculated that *-ago* came from the Latin verb *egere*, 'to lack, need or desire.' That, of course, is one *man*'s opinion.

The busiest branch of the *vir* family is the *virtue* bunch. Even in Latin, the root word *virtus* meant more than mere manliness. It also conveyed such exclusively male qualities as excellence, worth, industry, strength, valour, and courage, and most of these senses came along for the ride when *virtue* strode into the English language in the thirteenth century.

So worthy was this word that in one of its earliest English senses it denoted 'divine power,' and in some contexts was a synonym for 'miracle.' The prevailing sense, however, conveyed all that was good and righteous, free from vice or immorality. Eventually, even a woman could earn the right to possess virtue, if she could elevate her behaviour and thought to the high standards of the opposite sex. That's probably not what Proverbs 12:4 meant, however, in saying, 'A virtuous woman is a crown to her husband.' Here, the virtue was either chastity or devotion to 'womanly' duties.

The adjective *virtual* originally meant 'full of virtue,' but eventually came to mean 'in effect, but not in fact,' as it were. And that, I gather, is the virtue of virtual reality. I must try it soon, but lately I've been too busy trying to keep up with literal reality.

———————————   •   •   •   ———————————

The object of flyting was to poetically declare your opponent undeserving of existence. Kings were among its fans and targets. Modern rap just isn't in the same class.

THE 'EVILL' ZAP OF EARLY RAP

I'D BE THE LAST PERSON TO KNOCK RAP. IT'S JUST THAT WHEN I WANT to catch up on the socio-politico-ethno-culturo-macho-misogyno-narcissism scene, my tastes run more toward learned journals, like *Playboy* and *Hustler*. And I like to do it at my own pace, usually three-quarter time, rather than have it ack-acked at me from the throbbing bowels of a tinted-windowed missile cooling its wheels at a stop light.

Furthermore, I do not think it excessively fastidious of me to prefer my current affairs commentaries in something vaguely reminiscent of English, and to insist – if they must be in verse – that the expositor come up with something just a little less poetically licentious than rhyming both 'except' and 'help' with 'step.'

Apart from these tiny cavils, I have nothing but respect for rap 'music' and those who 'perform' it. After all, there is an honourable precedent for mind-numbing, metrical invective in my own ethnic background. It's called 'flyting,' or abusive poetry, and it was elevated to a national art form in Scotland in the fifteenth and sixteenth centuries.

The tradition is even older than that. The ancient Greeks had *logomachies* (*logos*, 'word'; *machy*, 'battle'), which could be arguments over the subtleties of words, or more hostile 'cursing combats.' Arab armies at one time were led into battle not by standard-bearers or buglers but by poets, hurling scurrilous but scannable slurs at the enemy. Maybe that's where the latter-day warrior, Mohammed Ali, got the idea.

The Anglo-Saxons also flirted with flyting (an Old English word meaning 'to contend or argue'). In the tenth-century poem *Battle of Maldon*, the

Danish and English chieftains engaged in splendid pre-bout vaunts and taunts.

The practice has existed in some form in many cultures. In the Caribbean, calypso, as well as an epic, extempore verse style known as 'toasting,' was originally a form of social analysis and political satire. American slaves brought with them from Africa a charming game called 'the dozens,' in which two opponents insulted each other – and often each other's mother and sisters – until one lost his temper and the game turned physical. The traducer with the longer fuse was, of course, the winner, although it must have been hard to work up a vigorous celebratory mood while nursing a painfully disarranged physiognomy. The name *dozens* probably came not from the numerical sense but from the American word *bulldoze*, originally *bulldose*, which meant a severe dose of the bullwhip.

These may have been precursors to the raunchy repartee known as rap, a product of the black US ghettos of the 1970s. It has become an industry, as a visit to any large record store will attest. Most of the products bear labels warning of potentially offensive 'lyrics' – a somewhat superfluous caution given the general unintelligibility of the relentless badinage.

Equally impenetrable is the Middle Scots tongue in which the truly virtuoso versions of flyting poetry were couched. This vitriolic versification flourished in Scotland from about 1450 to the late 1500s, and counted among its targets, fans, and practitioners Kings James V and VI.

The object was to debase an opponent by mocking his origins, questioning his morals and sexual adequacy, enumerating and grossly exaggerating his physical shortcomings, and generally declaring him utterly undeserving of existence. These flytes of deprecatory fancy were executed in elaborate and formal verse structures, and they were always waged between friends.

One of the foremost exponents was William Dunbar, whose poem *The Flyting of Dunbar and Kennedie* (1500) is probably the apotheosis (or rock bottom, depending on your taste) of the genre. At one point, Kennedie calls Dunbar 'a crabbit, scabbit, evill facit messan tyke, a schit but wit, schyre and injurius.' This translates to 'an ill-natured, scabrous, ugly lap-dog cur, a witless turd, meagre and malicious.'

Poet Robert Henryson's *Sum Practysis of Medecyne*, a scathing send-up of doctors, contains a prescription requiring a patient to sit in a pan of the most disgusting scatological ingredients while kissing the very private part of a cow.

For some reason Scottish verse flyting crash-landed in the 1580s, never to soar again. It was probably the victim of a bum rap.

———————————   •   •   •   ———————————

Common expressions often take a jumbled journey from obscurity to familiarity. We've come a long way 'down the pike' – a phrase that may now be going down the tubes.

PICKING A PECK OF PICKLED PIKES

R EGULAR READERS WILL KNOW THAT THE INCUMBENT SCRIBBLER has a soft spot for a phenomenon called 'folk' or 'popular' etymology, a fascinating process of word perversion in which obscure forms are replaced by more familiar ones while staying more or less in the same semantic ballpark. Thus the borrowed *chaise longue*, or 'long chair,' is well along the way to becoming *chaise lounge*, and *cole slaw* bids fair to becoming the apparently more logical *cold slaw*.

The old expression *coming down the pike* – meaning 'on the way,' 'in the offing,' 'on the cards,' or 'about to appear on the scene' – may be undergoing a similar charming corruption, in which the last word increasingly comes out as *pipe*.

A headline in this month's *Report on Business Magazine* said 'Coming down the pipe.' The story was about a gas pipeline company, but the pun was possible only because the headline writer knowingly or otherwise muddled two metaphors: *coming down the pike* and *in the pipeline*, both meaning roughly the same thing.

Unfortunately the new, mutant version, sometimes shortened to *down the pipe*, carries an almost opposite connotation. Something that's *down the pipe*, or imminent, can also be construed as *down the drain (pipe)* or, in a newer version, *down the tubes* – meaning finished, washed up, through, done for, defunct, like the Monty Python parrot.

Down the pike, however, just means *down the road*, since *pike* is a short form of *turnpike*, which is short for *turnpike road*. But its jumbled journey goes back a long way, providing a curious and captivating example of the convoluted evolution of word sense.

In Old English it was *pic*, probably pronounced with a long vowel as in *pipe*, and represented a simple tool for picking at the ground. In the fourteenth century, speakers began shortening the vowel, the result of which are today's *pickaxe* and the verb *pick*, meaning to select or cull something as with a pointed implement. The verb *peck* is another variant.

Meanwhile, *pike* was attaching itself to a variety of things whose common characteristic was some degree of pointiness. Through the ages, a *pike* has been a mountain, a weapon, a severely tapered shoe, the 'beak' of an anvil, the pin of a lathe, and a long-nosed fish whose diminutive is *pickerel*. But for vagrant eddies in the etymological stream, we might today use a tooth*pike* after eating *pick*ishly.

To confuse matters further, still another variation, *peak*, entered the language in the sixteenth century. At about the same time the English, not content with their own profusion of confusables, reached across the Channel and picked up the related French *piquer*, 'to sting, pierce or stimulate,' and formed their own *pique* and *piquancy*.

At some fork in the road, somebody put the words *turn* and *pike* together to describe a menacing spiked barrier placed across a road as a defence against raiders on horseback. Later this was mounted on a vertical axis and used to stop travellers until they paid a toll. Before long, any road that had these taxing turnstiles became known as a *turnpike road*, then a *turnpike*, and finally just a *pike*.

People who tramped along them were called *pikers*, a term that became synonymous with 'thieves,' who were also called *pickers*. New dimensions were added to *piker* in the mid-nineteenth century when a large number of wealth-seekers from Pike County, Missouri, joined the 1849 gold rush to California. They were reputedly timid at betting in card games, and *piker* came to mean 'cheapskate.'

That same gold fever attracted other prospectors to a Colorado mountain rumoured to contain rich lodes. The mountain, discovered and named by Zebulon Montgomery Pike, a US Army officer and explorer, was Pike's Peak, a topographical anomaly and an etymological redundancy.

Incidentally, Zeb Pike met his end in Canada. During the War of 1812, he led a raid against the British garrison at York, later called Hogtown and sometimes Toronto. The retreating Redcoats, in a fit of pique, set fire to their own powder magazine. In the resulting explosion, a large rock landed lethally on Pike's own peak. At which point, a pitiless Brit sneered: 'That's a come-down for Pike,' thus further confusing the issue.

———————————   •   •   •   ———————————

Here's one of our periodical surveys of slip-ups on the printed page, those dubious juxtapositions of bits of speech that give the reader a choice of two meanings, one of them humorous.

DANGLING ABSURDITIES: STILL HANGING IN

W HAT YOU SEE IS NOT ALWAYS WHAT YOU GET, IN PUBLIC PRINT. Reporters, headline writers, advertising hacks, and wordmongers of other stripes have an endearing way of stringing – or flinging – words together that often leaves them with egg on their typefaces.

Adjectives, adverbs, pronouns, participles, and other bits of speech are deployed in a hilariously helter-skelter manner, leaving the beholder with two or more choices of interpretation, at least one of which has a tendency to titillate. Faithful readers of this column (and I know who both of you are) will recall that I collect examples of these mirth-making malformations in a file tabbed 'Dangling Absurdities.'

It's been an eventful year since we last dipped into this dossier of doubtful-entendres. One event was the Summer Olympic Games, whose marathon race paled by comparison with other chronicled feats of superhuman stamina and endurance. *Press Review*, a quarterly magazine for journalists, reported on the freeing of American hostage Terry Anderson, whose plight apparently didn't get any better after his delivery from Lebanese captors into US hands. 'Anderson was Middle East Affairs Chief for Associated Press when he was dragged off the street, blindfolded and put in chains,' the magazine said. 'He still holds that position.'

In the long run, the Olympic marathon also had nothing on the job requirement contained in an ad in the Iowa City *Press-Citizen*, as reprinted in the *New Yorker*: 'Clear Creek High School needs a girl's varsity track coach to run from mid-March through end of May.'

That had me in stitches, but not as many as did this diagnosis quoted in a book called *The Best of Medical Humor*. 'Patient has chest pain if she lies on her left side for over a year.' There's probably another side to that story, as there likely is to this startling statistic reprinted in the *Communications Briefings* newsletter: 'About 235,000 Americans have their portraits taken by professional photographers every day.' I guess they just don't know when to stop.

Reader Eric Willis of Waterdown, Ontario, didn't realize he was in for a test of stick-to-it-iveness when he came to the final stage of a bathroom renovation. A large red-and-white label warned: 'Do not pull on grab bar after caulking for 24 hours.'

In exchange, Mr Willis, I pass on this related headline, used by Willard R. Espy in his book *The Word's Gotten Out*: 'Slipping and falling in bathtubs is often due to curved bottoms, it's said.'

Still, these people survived. Others were not so lucky. An Associated Press story provided a hitherto unknown historical detail in its lead paragraph: 'Spike Lee says his new movie "Malcolm X" ends in the townships of South Africa, not the Harlem ballroom where the black nationalist was assassinated for artistic reasons.'

If you think that's cruel and unusual punishment for abuse of artistic licence, how about this notice spotted by *Communications Briefings*: 'There will be an exhibition of art by Soviet artists executed over the past two years.'

Food brings out the best and worst of dangling absurdities. The *Globe and Mail*'s 'Cuisine' column gave this mouth-watering description of culinary creationism in Mennonite Ontario: 'Pigs and cattle are slaughtered in a communal effort to make farmers and summer sausage.'

If music be the food of love, miscues also figure on menus. A Los Angeles community newspaper served this notice: 'On Valentine's Day, Salisbury Manor is serving a $35 per person dinner which includes Chive Potato Crepes, Prime Rib, Lemon Sorbet and a harpist.' I hear the sorbet was heavenly, but the harpist was a bit stringy.

The world's your oyster, though, at Burger King, which started serving products in paper wrapping instead of boxes, in an effort to reduce waste. Calling it 'earth-happy packaging,' the fast-food chain added: 'It's just one of the ways we're trying to make the world a better place to eat.' For those with big appetites, no doubt.

My favourite of the past year is a one-liner that popped up on my electronic mail screen. It was the opening sentence of a message from a hard-working, and possibly desperate, United Way canvasser. It read: 'I'm selling United Way buttons as well as Rose-Mary Matusiak.'

———————————   •   •   •   ———————————

BIBLIOGRAPHY

Avis, Walter S., and Scargill, M.H. *A Dictionary of Canadianisms on Historical Principles.* Toronto: W.J. Gage, 1967.

Barnette, Martha. *A Garden of Words.* New York: Times Books, 1992.

Baugh, Albert C., and Cable, Thomas. *A History of the English Language.* 3rd edition. Englewood Cliffs, NJ: Prentice-Hall, 1978.

Berlitz, Charles. *Native Tongues.* New York: Grosset and Dunlap, 1982.

Bett, Henry. *Wanderings among Words.* London: George Allen & Unwin, 1936.

Brewer, Rev. E. Cobham. *Dictionary of Phrase and Fable.* London: Galley Press. A reproduction of the 1894 original.

Copley, J. *Shift of Meaning.* Oxford: Oxford University Press, 1961.

Drabble, Margaret. *Oxford Companion to English Literature.* 5th edition. Oxford: Oxford University Press, 1985.

Enright, D.J. *Fair of Speech – The Uses of Euphemism.* Oxford: Oxford University Press, 1985.

Espy, Willard R. *The Word's Gotten Out.* New York: Clarkson N. Potter, 1989.

Fowler, H.W. *A Dictionary of Modern English Usage.* Oxford: Oxford University Press, 1926.

Grose, Francis. *A Classical Dictionary of the Vulgar Tongue.* New York: Dorset Press, 1992. First published in 1796.

Hail, J.R. Clark. *A Concise Anglo-Saxon Dictionary.* 4th edition. Toronto: University of Toronto Press 1991. First published in 1894.

Heller, Louis G.; Humez, Alexander; and Dror, Malach. *The Private Lives of English Words.* New York: Wynwood Press, 1991.

Johnson, Samuel. *A Dictionary of the English Language.* London: Longman. A facsimile reproduction of the original 1755 edition.

Kuiper, Kathleen. *Merriam-Webster's Encyclopedia of Literature*. Springfield, Mass.: Merriam-Webster, 1995.

Lewis, C.T., and Short, Charles. *A Latin Dictionary*. Oxford: Oxford University Press, 1993.

McAdam, E.L. Jr., and Milne, George. *Johnson's Dictionary: A Modern Selection*. New York: Pantheon Books, 1963.

McArthur, Tom. *Oxford Companion to the English Language*. Oxford: Oxford University Press, 1992.

McDonald, James. *Wordly Wise*. London: Constable, 1984.

McKay, Charles. *Lost Beauties of the English Language*. London: Bibliophile Books, 1987. First published in 1874.

Mellinkoff, David. *The Language of the Law*. 7th printing. Boston and Toronto: Little Brown, 1990.

Mencken, H.L. *The American Language*. 4th edition. New York: Alfred A. Knopf, 1937.

Murray, K.M. Elisabeth. *Caught in the Web of Words – James Murray and the Oxford English Dictionary*. Oxford: Oxford University Press, 1979.

Nurnberg, Maxwell. *I Always Look Up the Word 'Egregious.'* Englewood Cliffs, NJ: Prentice-Hall, 1981.

Oxford English Dictionary. 2nd edition. Oxford: Oxford University Press, 1989.

Palmer, Rev. A. Smythe. *Folk-Etymology: A Dictionary of Verbal Corruptions of Words Perverted in Form or Meaning, by False Derivation or Mistaken Analogy*. New York: Greenwood Press, 1969. First published in 1883.

Partridge, Eric. *A Short Etymological Dictionary of Modern English*. New York: Greenwich House, 1983.

Ray, John. *A Collection of English Words Not Generally Used*. Aldershot, England: Scholar Press, 1969. First published in 1674.

Skeat, W.W. *Etymological Dictionary of the English Language*. 4th edition. Oxford: Clarendon Press 1910.

Thomas, Lewis. *Et Cetera – Notes of a Word-Watcher*. Toronto: Little Brown, 1990.

Trench, Richard Chenevix. *A Select Glossary of English Words, Used Formerly in Senses Different from Their Present*. 2nd edition. London: John Parker, 1859.

– *On the Study of Words: English Past and Present ['Supplée's Trench on Words']*. New York: A.C. Armstrong and Son, 1893.

Urdang, Laurence. *Three-Toed Sloths & Seven-League Boots; A Dictionary of Numerical Expressions*. New York: Barnes & Noble, 1992.

Warrack, Alexander. *Chambers Scots Dictionary*. Edinburg: W. & R. Chambers, 1987 reprint.

Watkins, Calvert, ed. *The American Heritage Dictionary of Indo-European Roots*. Boston: Houghton Mifflin, 1985.

Webster's *Dictionary of English Usage*. Springfield, Mass: Merriam Webster Inc., 1989.

Weekley, Ernest. *Adjectives and Other Words*. Freeport, NY: Books for Libraries Press, 1970. First published in 1930.

— *An Etymological Dictionary of Modern English*. 2 volumes. Toronto: General Publishing, 1967. First published in 1921.

— *More Words Ancient and Modern*. Freeport, NY: Books for Libraries Press, 1971. First published in 1927.

— *Romance of Words*. 5th edition. London: John Murray, 1925.

— *Something about Words*. London: John Murray, 1935.

— *Words Ancient and Modern*. London: John Murray, 1926.

— *Words and Names*. Freeport, NY: Books for Libraries Press, 1971. First published in 1932.

INDEX

Words and phrases discussed in the book are in *italics*. General subjects are in ordinary *roman* with an initial capital letter. The proper names of people mentioned in the text are in **bold**.